Shelley's LEARNING ADVENTURES in NYC

75 Amazing Destinations to Explore!

250 East 54th Street, Suite P2
New York, NY 10022
www.lightswitchlearning.com
Copyright © 2020 Lightswitch Learning

Educators and Librarians, for a variety of teaching resources,
visit www.lightswitchlearning.com

Library of Congress Cataloging-in-Publication Data is available upon request.

ISBN: 978-1-68265-634-1

Shelley's LEARNING ADVENTURES In NYC

Design and Production: Paula Jo Smith
The text of this book is set in Trade Gothic and Billy
Printed in China

To my sons Matt and Ben and to the many schoolchildren in New York City, thank you for inspiring me to uncover so many magical learning adventures for families to discover and explore.

Contents

more ▶

Introduction

I'm Shelley Goldberg, and people are always stopping me on the street to ask me, "Where can I go with my children in New York City that's both educationally enriching and great fun?" That's because for close to twenty-five years, as the Parenting/Family Reporter for NY1 News, I reported on thousands of great educational experiences for families with children of all ages to enjoy throughout the five boroughs.

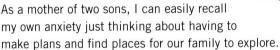
At the National Museum of Mathematics

As a mother of two sons, I can easily recall my own anxiety just thinking about having to make plans and find places for our family to explore.

In fact, this stress was exactly what inspired me to create the "Parenting Report" and the "Where To Go" segment on NY1 News. In addition, the feedback we received from our viewers further confirmed that we were ALL overwhelmed trying to decide where to go with our children!

What I discovered as a reporter, and a former teacher, was that finding great educational activities—what I call "Learning Adventures" for your family—need not be stressful. So, I've personally selected 75 great NYC places for learning adventures that cover a wide range of interests, from dinosaurs and dance and distant galaxies to ziplining and amazing math activities!

Each of these 75 places has the potential to help your children to identify their interests and passions, spark a new hobby, and even to discover their unique career paths! For example, going to a live theater performance may ignite an interest in costume design or choreography. An excursion to a science museum may supercharge a lifelong interest in aerodynamics or marine science. In fact, so powerful are these "learning adventures" in their ability to change young lives, that one of my sons was so fascinated by the architecture of Grand Central Station as a young boy, he decided on a career in the real estate industry.

But most important of all, these family outings will inspire you to become a researcher for great learning adventures, to step outside of your community to create wonderful learning opportunities and memories for your family throughout the five boroughs here in New York City.

So, let's get started!

How To Use This Book

Because every child is different, I decided not to recommend a specific age group for each learning adventure. Parents and guardians often know what is age-appropriate for their children. These 75 venues were chosen because they appeal to a variety of learning styles. From climbing in a science playground, to hearing young jazz musicians, to a quiet walk in the woods, there's something in this book for every style and type of learner, of all ages!

As you plan, always explore the specific website for each venue with your child and use its information to help plan your learning adventures. And please note that hours of operation and venue events are subject to change. Please check online or call ahead to confirm.

① General Information

Makes planning easy with admission, hours, how to get there, and links to special needs information and programs.

② Quick Online Links

Enables quick access via QR code to each venue's website. To access the QR code download a QR code reader app from either an iPhone or Android phone.

③ SHELLEY REPORTS

Offers my recommendations for cool and interesting activities to help focus your learning adventures at every venue!

④ More Info

Includes updates and highlights for special events, activities, and exhibits that will be occurring at each venue throughout the year.

AFRICAN BURIAL GROUND NATIONAL MONUMENT
290 Broadway, Manhattan, (212) 637-2019
VISIT: nps.gov/afbg/index.htm

③ **SHELLEY REPORTS**

This is the site of NYC's earliest known African burial ground, discovered to include more than 400 free and enslaved men, women, and children.

① **ADMISSION**
Free

HOURS
TUES.–SAT. 10 AM–4 PM

HOW TO GET HERE
Subway:
Ⓐ Ⓒ Ⓙ Ⓡ Ⓩ
① ② ③ ④ ⑤ ⑥
Bus: M9 X1 X10 X28

FOR SPECIAL NEEDS
lslearn.info/afburial

- **WORK OF ENSLAVED AFRICANS EXHIBIT** From household chores to the backbreaking labor of moving cargo, explore the daily work of enslaved men and women in this eye-opening display.
- **VISITOR CENTER** Through re-creations, videos, and photos, discover moving stories of the African people who were enslaved in NYC until the mid-1800s.
- **OUTSIDE MEMORIAL** With tall granite slabs angled to look like the hull of a ship, this tribute memorializes the 15,000 Africans buried in Lower Manhattan.
- **"OUR TIME AT LAST"** This informative video tells a fictionalized story of an enslaved girl in the 1700s, while also exploring the history of the burial ground's discovery.

② ④ MORE INFO: **ShelleysLearningAdventures.com**

SHELLEY'S ACTIVITIES

Parents are always looking for ways to support and enhance the learning that goes on in the classroom so that their children have the best chance to be successful. Here's a simple 4-step learning plan to give you the confidence and guidance you need before, during, and after each learning adventure:

1 LET'S GET STARTED Learn new vocabulary words to build background knowledge and improve academic language.

2 ON THE WAY Ignite curiosity beforehand with critical thinking questions that inspire discussion and discovery.

3 NOW YOU ARE HERE Participate in a variety of activities—including social media—to share with family and friends and classmates, too.

4 ON THE WAY HOME Discuss and analyze questions to improve conceptual understanding of key content concepts.

DID YOU KNOW? Get inspired with amazing facts and data designed to enhance each learning adventure.

 Investigate and develop the skills and training necessary to inspire career and life success.

 Explore more learning adventures in the neighborhood within approximately one mile of the selected venue.

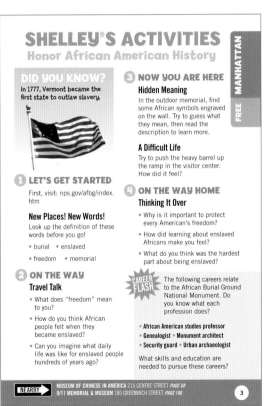

SHELLEY'S ACTIVITIES
Honor African American History

DID YOU KNOW?
In 1777, Vermont became the first state to outlaw slavery.

1 LET'S GET STARTED
First, visit: nps.gov/afbg/index.htm

New Places! New Words!
Look up the definition of these words before you go!
• burial • enslaved
• freedom • memorial

2 ON THE WAY
Travel Talk
• What does "freedom" mean to you?
• How do you think African people felt when they became enslaved?
• Can you imagine what daily life was like for enslaved people hundreds of years ago?

3 NOW YOU ARE HERE
Hidden Meaning
In the outdoor memorial, find some African symbols engraved on the wall. Try to guess what they mean, then read the description to learn more.

A Difficult Life
Try to push the heavy barrel up the ramp in the visitor center. How did it feel?

4 ON THE WAY HOME
Thinking It Over
• Why is it important to protect every American's freedom?
• How did learning about enslaved Africans make you feel?
• What do you think was the hardest part about being enslaved?

CAREER FLASH
The following careers relate to the African Burial Ground National Monument. Do you know what each profession does?
• African American studies professor
• Genealogist • Monument architect
• Security guard • Urban archaeologist
What skills and education are needed to pursue these careers?

FREE MANHATTAN

NEARBY ▶ MUSEUM OF CHINESE IN AMERICA 215 CENTRE STREET *PAGE 68*
9/11 MEMORIAL & MUSEUM 180 GREENWICH STREET *PAGE 100*

3

more ▶

Tab Information

TIVITIES
can History

)W YOU ARE HERE

den Meaning
he outdoor memorial, find
he African symbols engraved
the wall. Try to guess what
y mean, then read the
cription to learn more.

MANHATTAN

FREE

Choose a Borough: Select your learning adventures by borough.

Choose a Venue/Price: Choose a venue with prices that fit your budget. Prices here are the average adult ticket price.

★	Pay-What-You-Wish/Suggested Admission
FREE	No entrance fee
$	One adult ticket is between $1–$15.
$$	One adult ticket is between $16–$30.
$$$	One adult ticket is between $31–$45.
$$$$	One adult ticket is between $46–$60.
$$$$+	One adult ticket is $61 or more.

Admission Information

Please note the following admission prices when choosing venues:

Pay What You Wish/Suggested Admission: You need to pay something for admission, but you get to decide exactly how much you'd like to pay! How cool is that!

Varied Performances: Some venues like Teatro SEA _(pages 130-131)_ present many different kinds of performances and shows. Visit the venue website for specific prices for various events.

Additional Learning Adventure Fees

A venue may be marked "FREE" but there are additional activities available at the site for a fee. For example, Pelham Bay Park _(pages 102-103)_ is FREE, but to play miniature golf, there will be a cost. Visit the venue website for specific prices for various activities.

Also, here are several initiatives and programs that provide FREE admission to many of the learning adventures listed in this guide:

Culture Pass: Brooklyn Public Library, New York Public Library, and Queens Library cardmembers can make reservations for FREE visits to many cultural attractions. Visit: **www.culturepass.nyc/**

IDNYC Museum & Cultural Pass: New York City residents age 10 and older can get receive a pass for free access to museums and other cultural institutions. Visit: **www1.nyc.gov/site/idnyc/benefits/museums-and-cultural-institutions.page**

Cool Culture Family Pass: Provides free unlimited, admission to many cultural institutions. Visit: **www.coolculture.org/parents/cool-culture-family-guide**

FREE and Pay What You Wish on Special Days!

Some venues are FREE. But for those that have an admission fee, many have special days and times when admission for the venue is FREE including:

TUESDAYS:
- 9/11 MEMORIAL AND MUSEUM: 5–8 PM
  (Last admission is 2 hours prior to closing.)

WEDNESDAYS:
- MUSEUM OF JEWISH HERITAGE: 4–8 PM
- NEW YORK BOTANICAL GARDEN: 10 AM–5 PM
- NEW YORK AQUARIUM: 3–4:30 PM
- BRONX ZOO: 10 AM–4:30 PM
- STATEN ISLAND CHILDREN'S MUSEUM:
  5–8 PM (Jul.–Aug.), 3–5 PM (Sep.–Jun.)

THURSDAYS:
- BROOKLYN CHILDREN'S MUSEUM: 2–6 PM
- CHILDREN'S MUSEUM OF THE ARTS: 4–6 PM
- MUSEUM OF CHINESE IN AMERICA: 11 AM–9 PM
  (1st Thursday of the Month)
- MUSEUM OF JEWISH HERITAGE: 4–8 PM

FRIDAYS:
- HISTORIC RICHMOND TOWN: 1–5 PM
- MUSEUM OF THE MOVING IMAGE: 4–8 PM
- NEW YORK HALL OF SCIENCE: 2–5 PM
- NEW-YORK HISTORICAL SOCIETY: 6–9 PM

SATURDAYS:
- NEW YORK BOTANICAL GARDEN: 9–10 AM
- SOLOMON R. GUGGENHEIM MUSEUM: 5–7:45 PM (last ticket at 7:15)

SUNDAYS:
- BROOKLYN CHILDREN'S MUSEUM: 4–7 PM
- NEW YORK HALL OF SCIENCE: 10–11 AM
- SUGAR HILL CHILDREN'S MUSEUM OF ART & STORYTELLING:
  10 AM–5 PM (3rd Sundays of the Month)

AFRICAN BURIAL GROUND NATIONAL MONUMENT

290 Broadway, Manhattan, (212) 637-2019
VISIT: nps.gov/afbg/index.htm

SHELLEY REPORTS

This is the site of NYC's earliest known African burial ground, discovered to include more than 400 free and enslaved men, women, and children.

ADMISSION
Free

HOURS
TUES.–SAT. 10 AM–4 PM

HOW TO GET HERE
Subway:
A C J R Z
1 2 3 4 5 6
Bus: M9 X1 X10 X28

FOR SPECIAL NEEDS
lslearn.info/afburial

- **WORK OF ENSLAVED AFRICANS EXHIBIT** From household chores to the backbreaking labor of moving cargo, explore the daily work of enslaved men and women in this eye-opening display.

- **VISITOR CENTER** Through re-creations, videos, and photos, discover moving stories of the African people who were enslaved in NYC until the mid-1800s.

- **OUTSIDE MEMORIAL** With tall granite slabs angled to look like the hull of a ship, this tribute memorializes the 15,000 Africans buried in Lower Manhattan.

- **"OUR TIME AT LAST"** This informative video tells a fictionalized story of an enslaved girl in the 1700s, while also exploring the history of the burial ground's discovery.

SHELLEY'S ACTIVITIES
Honor African American History

DID YOU KNOW?

In 1777, Vermont became the first state to outlaw slavery.

1 LET'S GET STARTED

First, visit: nps.gov/afbg/index. htm

New Places! New Words!

Look up the definition of these words before you go!

- burial
- enslaved
- freedom
- memorial

2 ON THE WAY
Travel Talk

- What does "freedom" mean to you?
- How do you think African people felt when they became enslaved?
- Can you imagine what daily life was like for enslaved people hundreds of years ago?

3 NOW YOU ARE HERE
Hidden Meaning

In the outdoor memorial, find some African symbols engraved on the wall. Try to guess what they mean, then read the description to learn more.

A Difficult Life

Try to push the heavy barrel up the ramp in the visitor center. How did it feel?

4 ON THE WAY HOME
Thinking It Over

- Why is it important to protect every American's freedom?
- How did learning about enslaved Africans make you feel?
- What do you think was the hardest part about being enslaved?

CAREER FLASH

The following careers relate to the African Burial Ground National Monument. Do you know what each profession does?

- African American studies professor
- Genealogist • Monument architect
- Security guard • Urban archaeologist

What skills and education are needed to pursue these careers?

NEARBY ▶ MUSEUM OF CHINESE IN AMERICA 215 CENTRE STREET *PAGE 68*
9/11 MEMORIAL & MUSEUM 180 GREENWICH STREET *PAGE 100*

AMERICAN MUSEUM OF NATURAL HISTORY

79th Street & Central Park West, Manhattan,
(212) 769-5100   VISIT: amnh.org

ADMISSION
General Admission:
Pay what you wish.

To see all exhibits:
Children *(2–12)*: $20
Students *(with ID)*: $27
Adults: $33
Seniors *(60+)*: $27

HOURS
DAILY 10 AM–5:45 PM

HOW TO GET HERE
Subway: Ⓑ Ⓒ ➊

Bus: M7 M10 M11
M79 M86 M104

FOR SPECIAL NEEDS
lslearn.info/amnh

SHELLEY REPORTS

From dinosaurs to life-size dioramas, we're traveling back millions of years then moving into the future! Science meets history at this awesome museum!

- **DINOSAURS** You'll meet a huge Barosaurus protecting its baby from a scary Allosaurus when you first arrive. Then head up to the fourth floor for more.

- **BLUE WHALE** How about an enormous Blue Whale hanging from the ceiling on the first floor? It's impossible to miss!

- **LIFE-SIZE DIORAMAS** There are amazing dioramas that house life-size mammals on the first, second, and third floors. Don't miss these!

- **ROSE CENTER FOR EARTH AND SPACE** Explore the 13-billion-year history of the universe including Earth, other planets, and galaxies far, far away.

MORE INFO: **ShelleysLearningAdventures.com**

SHELLEY'S ACTIVITIES
Our Universe All in One Museum!

DID YOU KNOW?
Most dinosaurs were vegetarians! They ate plants and parts of trees.

③ NOW YOU ARE HERE

Instagram Fun!
Take plenty of pics in front of the enormous dinosaurs and life-size elephants!

That Whale Is So Big!
Walk around the Blue Whale a few times and see if you can guess how long it is.

① LET'S GET STARTED
First, visit: amnh.org

New Places! New Words!
Look up the definition of these words before you go!

- biomes
- habitat
- mammal
- meteorite
- solar system

④ ON THE WAY HOME

Thinking It Over
- How do you think dinosaurs communicated with each other?
- What different planets have you seen? In what ways are they alike? How are they different?

② ON THE WAY

Travel Talk
- Why do you think dinosaurs disappeared from Earth?
- What planets are part of our solar system?
- Is a whale considered a fish? Why or why not?

CAREER FLASH

The following careers help support museums. Do you know what each profession does?

- Bioinformatics manager
- Conservator • Curator
- Paleontologist

Pick careers to research. What skills and education do you need to pursue these careers?

NEARBY → **CENTRAL PARK** ENTER ON 77TH OR 81ST STREET *PAGE 20*
NEW-YORK HISTORICAL SOCIETY 170 CENTRAL PARK WEST *PAGE 94*

5

APOLLO THEATER

253 W. 125th Street, Manhattan,
(212) 531-5300   VISIT: apollotheater.org

ADMISSION
Weekday tours: $17
Weekend tours: $19

HOURS
Tours must be booked
in advance. Call
Mr. Billy Mitchell, tour
director, (212) 531-5337.

SHOW ADMISSION
Show prices and
times vary. Check
apollotheater.org.

HOW TO GET HERE
Subway: (A)(B)(C)(D)
(2)(3)(4)(5)(6)

Bus: M10 M100 M101
M104 M2 Bx15

FOR SPECIAL NEEDS
Wheelchair accessible

SHELLEY REPORTS

Wow! So many musical legends
and entertainers have appeared on
this stage in Harlem. Discover the
incredible history of the Apollo
Theater by taking a backstage tour!

- **HISTORIC TOUR** Take a special backstage tour of this
famous theater! Try to call tour director Billy Mitchell at
least a week in advance to reserve your spot.

- **THE WALL OF SIGNATURES** As part of the tour,
spot signatures of the famous people who have visited
or performed at the Apollo—including Barack Obama
and John Legend!

- **TAKE THE STAGE** Imagine you're an artist in the
Apollo spotlight! On the tour, follow famous footsteps by
walking on the stage and touring dressing rooms.

- **AMATEUR NIGHT** Once a week, the Apollo hosts a
search for new, exciting talent. Check the calendar to
buy tickets to this famous show!

SHELLEY'S ACTIVITIES
Discover Where Stars Are Born!

DID YOU KNOW?

Music superstars Stevie Wonder, Lauryn Hill, and Ne-Yo all got their start at Apollo's Amateur Night.

③ NOW YOU ARE HERE

Feeling Lucky?
Snap a selfie rubbing the Apollo's famous Tree of Hope!

So Many Signatures!
How many names do you recognize on the Wall of Signatures?

① LET'S GET STARTED

First, visit: apollotheater.org

New Places! New Words!
Look up the definition of these words before you go!

- amateur
- audition
- contestant
- melody

④ ON THE WAY HOME

Thinking It Over

- In addition to a unique voice, what other talents must a singer have?
- If you could meet anyone who has performed at the Apollo, who would it be?
- What do you think are all the different emotions a performer feels on stage?

② ON THE WAY

Travel Talk

- If you could sing, dance, or perform comedy at the Apollo, which would you choose?
- Which performer would you like to see on the stage of the Apollo and why?
- What words would you include in a song about your life?

CAREER FLASH

The following careers relate to the Apollo Theater. Do you know what each profession does?

- **Audio and video technician**
- **Box office manager** • **Lighting director**
- **Social media marketer** • **Talent agent**

Pick jobs to research. What skills and education are needed to pursue these careers?

BAMkids

30 Lafayette Avenue, Brooklyn, (various other venue sites)
(718) 636-4100 x1   VISIT: bam.org/kids

ADMISSION

Ticket prices vary by performance. Discounts available for children. Check the website for dates, times, and tickets.

HOW TO GET HERE

Subway:

B C D G N Q
R 2 3 4 5

Bus: B25 B26 B41 B45 B52 B63 B67

FOR SPECIAL NEEDS

lslearn.info/bamkids

SHELLEY REPORTS

You never know what performances you'll find at BAMkids! From an interactive tech experience to hip-hop events, it's always a new adventure for children of all ages!

- **MUSIC, DANCE, THEATER!** Fun concerts, amazing acrobatics, and rockin' robots are just some of the diverse lineup of amazing performances offered.

- **MOVIE MATINEES** BAMkids hosts films for movie lovers on select Sundays, from animated classics to musicals and international fare.

- **CALENDAR** Check the online calendar for updates about movies, concerts, a cool February film festival, and theatrical shows that bring the magic of stagecraft alive!

MORE INFO: **ShelleysLearningAdventures.com**

SHELLEY'S ACTIVITIES
Music, Movies, and Dance!

DID YOU KNOW?

The playwright Lin-Manuel Miranda first performed a song from his hit musical *Hamilton* at a White House Poetry Jam party.

③ NOW YOU ARE HERE

Improvise a Poem!

After the event, create a spoken word poem about the show. Share it with your friends or family!

Dream Up a Movie!

Come up with a one-line description of an exciting movie plot, starring you!

① LET'S GET STARTED

First, visit: bam.org/kids

New Places! New Words!

Look up the definition of these words before you go!

- beatboxing • cinephile
- humanities
- spoken word poetry

② ON THE WAY

Travel Talk

- Which movie character do you relate to most? Why?
- How does a mime or clown make people laugh without ever talking?
- What attributes do hip-hop lyrics and poetry have in common?

④ ON THE WAY HOME

Thinking It Over

- How can you make music without an instrument or your voice?
- How are animated films different than live-action films?
- Analyze the different ways lighting is used in a performance to show different moods.

CAREER FLASH

The following careers relate to BAMkids. Do you know what each profession does?

- **Choreographer** • **Manager of venue sales**
- **Theatrical electrician**

Pick careers to research. What skills and education are needed to pursue these careers?

BRONX ZOO

2300 Southern Boulevard, Bronx, (718) 220-5100

VISIT: bronxzoo.com

ADMISSION

Children *(under 3)*: Free
Children *(3–12)*: $14.95
Adults *(13+)*: $22.95
Seniors *(65+)*: $20.95
Special exhibits are additional costs.

HOURS

NOV.–MAR.
10 AM–4:30 PM
WEEKDAYS APR.–OCT.
10 AM–5 PM
WEEKENDS & HOLIDAYS APR.–OCT.
10 AM–5:30 PM

HOW TO GET HERE

Subway: **2**

Bus: Bx9 Bx12 Bx19 Bx22 BxM11 Q44

FOR SPECIAL NEEDS

lslearn.info/bxzoo

SHELLEY REPORTS

Lions, tigers, and bears! Oh my! With more than 650 species, the Bronx Zoo is truly a world of diversity, wonder, and awe. You won't believe you're in the Bronx!

- **FEEDING TIME!** At select times every day, watch zookeepers feed fish and marine life to eager sea lions and bobbing Magellanic penguins.

- **CHILDREN'S ZOO** During warmer months, don't pass up the chance to pet alpacas, mini Nubian goats, and sheep.

- **BUG CAROUSEL** Take a spin on this whimsical ride. Hop on a giant praying mantis, grasshopper, or dung beetle instead of a horse!

- **WILD ASIA MONORAIL** Spot elephants, rhinos, Asian deer, and more from high above! Open during warmer months.

MORE INFO: **ShelleysLearningAdventures.com**

SHELLEY'S ACTIVITIES
Amazing Animals, Big and Small!

DID YOU KNOW?

There are more than 100,000 hissing cockroaches in the Madagascar! exhibit. They can grow up to 4 inches long!

① LET'S GET STARTED

First, visit: bronxzoo.com

New Places! New Words!
Look up the definition of these words before you go!

- biodiversity • endangered
- habitat • prey

② ON THE WAY
Travel Talk

- Why do some animal species become endangered or extinct?
- How do zoos protect animals and help support threatened species?

③ NOW YOU ARE HERE
Photo Scrapbook
Take photos in front of different animals. Create a scrapbook of your outing!

What Does It Eat?
As you explore the zoo, guess what each animal eats. Ask a zookeeper for the answer!

④ ON THE WAY HOME
Thinking It Over

- What part of a zookeeper's job would be the most difficult? What would be the most fun?
- How do zoos make each animal's habitat safe and comfortable?
- What is the difference between an omnivore, carnivore, and herbivore?

CAREER FLASH

The following careers relate to the Bronx Zoo. Do you know what each profession does?

- **Conservation biologist**
- **Curator of mammals** • **Herpetologist**
- **Veterinarian** • **Zookeeper**

Pick careers to research. What skills and education are needed to pursue these careers?

NEARBY → BRONX ZOO TREETOP ADVENTURE BRONX RIVER PKWY AT BOSTON ROAD *PAGE 12*
NEW YORK BOTANICAL GARDEN 2900 SOUTHERN BOULEVARD *PAGE 86*

BRONX ZOO TREETOP ADVENTURE

Bronx River Parkway at Boston Road, Bronx,
(347) 308-9021

VISIT: bronxzootreetop.com

ADMISSION
Zipline: $24.95
Climb: $49.95
Climb and Zipline:
$59.95

*Must be 7+ to participate.
See website for other
admission requirements.*

HOURS
Open Year-Round
(Weather Permitting)
Hours vary by season.
Call or visit website to
see updated hours.

HOW TO GET HERE
Subway: ②

Bus: BxM11

FOR SPECIAL NEEDS
lslearn.info/bxttop

SHELLEY REPORTS

Climb high into the trees for an awesome adventure! Take the ropes course challenge and then zipline across the Bronx River!

- **ZIPLINE** Strap into a harness and zoom over the forest canopy high above the Bronx River in this super exciting ride. It's a thrilling experience for nature lovers!

- **EXPLORE THE ROPES** Seven different ropes courses, ranging from easy to difficult, make this a jaw-dropping, unforgettable adventure. Don't worry—guides are there to cheer you on and help you!

- **TREETOP ADVENTURE AT NIGHT** Experience the delight of climbing and zipping through the air in the dark. The park is illuminated by lights, creating an incredible atmosphere for the adrenaline lovers among us!

MORE INFO: **ShelleysLearningAdventures.com**

SHELLEY'S ACTIVITIES
Zipline and Ropes Course Fun!

DID YOU KNOW?

Wildlife biologists in Costa Rica have used ziplines to study rainforests without bothering animals, like this three-toed sloth.

③ NOW YOU ARE HERE
So Many Obstacles!
How many ropes courses can you get through successfully?

Climbing Pics!
Have someone on the ground take a photo of you on the ropes course. See how brave you look!

① LET'S GET STARTED
First, visit: bronxzootreetop.com

New Places! New Words!
Look up the definition of these words before you go!

- carabiner
- forest canopy
- harness
- obstacle

④ ON THE WAY HOME
Thinking It Over
- What problems did you have to solve when climbing the ropes course?
- How do zipline designers ensure that people who participate are safe?

② ON THE WAY
Travel Talk
- What can you see from above a forest that you can't see from the ground?
- Why do people enjoy thrilling experiences like ziplining?
- If you wanted to design a ropes course, what might you need to study?

CAREER FLASH

The following careers relate to the Bronx Zoo Treetop Adventure. Do you know what each profession does?

- Canopy ecologist
- Manufacturing assembly specialist
- Ropes course designer • Safety inspector
- Structural engineer

Pick careers to research. What skills and education are needed to pursue these careers?

BROOKLYN CHILDREN'S MUSEUM

145 Brooklyn Avenue, Brooklyn, (718) 735-4400
VISIT: brooklynkids.org

SHELLEY REPORTS

This is a magical place in Brooklyn for children and families. With three floors of hands-on interactive exhibits, get ready to engage in scientific exploration and discovery.

ADMISSION
Children *(under 1)*: Free
General Admission: $11

HOURS
TUES., WED., FRI.
10 AM–5 PM
THUR. 10 AM–6 PM
SAT.–SUN. 10 AM–7 PM

HOW TO GET HERE
Subway: Ⓐ Ⓒ ③

Bus: B25 B43 B44
B45 B65

FOR SPECIAL NEEDS
Wheelchair accessible

- **BROOKLYN BLOCK LAB** With language blocks in English, Hebrew, and even American Sign Language, this space makes block play fascinating for all ages.

- **WORLD BROOKLYN** Pretend to be a shopkeeper, a baker, or a customer in child-sized stores—all inspired by Brooklyn's international bakeries and grocery stores!

- **COLLECTIONS CENTRAL** From fossils to Native American artifacts, explore objects from the museum's incredible collection of 29,000 scientific and cultural items.

- **NEIGHBORHOOD NATURE** Learn about Brooklyn's creatures and plants! Harvest plants, study habitats— even touch crabs and sea stars!

MORE INFO: **ShelleysLearningAdventures.com**

SHELLEY'S ACTIVITIES
Play, Plant, and Learn!

DID YOU KNOW?

America's first roller coaster opened in Brooklyn in 1884.

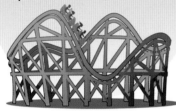

① LET'S GET STARTED

First, visit: brooklynkids.org

New Places! New Words!

Look up the definition of these words before you go!

- conservator
- habitat
- international
- minerals

② ON THE WAY

Travel Talk

- How do museums teach science and history without using textbooks?
- What can you learn about different cultures from the foods they prepare?
- Why is it so important to take care of our environment and the world we live in?

③ NOW YOU ARE HERE

Shop Snap!

In World Brooklyn, snap a selfie as a shopkeeper, baker, or chef!

Field Scientist

Using the museum's cameras and listening devices, discover animals hidden within the Neighborhood Nature dioramas!

④ ON THE WAY HOME

Thinking It Over

- Why is it helpful to see and touch something to learn about it?
- What math skills are needed to run a restaurant?
- What did the Neighborhood Nature area teach you about Brooklyn's environment?

CAREER FLASH The following careers relate to the Brooklyn Children's Museum. Do you know what each profession does?

- Botanist • Curriculum developer
- Marine biologist • Pastry chef
- Produce clerk

Pick careers to research. What skills and education are needed to pursue these careers?

NEARBY ▶ **BROOKLYN MUSEUM** 200 EASTERN PARKWAY *PAGE 16*

BROOKLYN MUSEUM
200 Eastern Parkway, Brooklyn, (718) 638-5000
VISIT: brooklynmuseum.org

ADMISSION
Suggested Admission:
Children *(under 20)*: Free
Students: $10
Adults: $16
Seniors *(65+)*: $10
Visitors with
disabilities: $2

HOURS
WED., FRI., SAT., SUN.
11 AM–6 PM
THUR. 11 AM–10 PM

HOW TO GET HERE
Subway: B D N Q
R 2 3

Bus: B41 B45 B69

FOR SPECIAL NEEDS
lslearn.info/bklynmus

SHELLEY REPORTS

> This museum is huge! Check out the large collection of Egyptian, American, African, and Asian art. It's a great way to learn about the world's many cultures.

- **ANCIENT EGYPT** Get up close to the museum's world-famous collection of Egyptian artifacts, including golden statuettes, ivory tools, and a mummy tomb beautifully painted in bright colors. They're fascinating!

- **GREAT ROOMS** Explore life long ago by walking through 23 decorated rooms from different time periods throughout American history.

- **VISIBLE STORAGE** The museum's permanent collection is gigantic! See more of its historical pieces, including ancient carved figures, ceramics, and miniature paintings from the 1700s.

MORE INFO: **ShelleysLearningAdventures.com**

SHELLEY'S ACTIVITIES
A World of Art in Brooklyn!

DID YOU KNOW?

Built by ancient Egyptians, the Great Pyramid of Giza weighs as much as 16 Empire State Buildings!

① LET'S GET STARTED

First, visit: brooklynmuseum.org

New Places! New Words!
Look up the definition of these words before you go!

- art deco
- ceramics
- civilization
- hieroglyph

② ON THE WAY
Travel Talk

- How were pyramids built without the use of modern technology?
- In what ways did electricity improve people's lives at home and at work?

③ NOW YOU ARE HERE
How Did They Use This?
In the Decorative Arts area, choose an object you don't recognize. What is its intended purpose?

Find a Cat!
Look for cats in ancient Egyptian artwork or sculptures. Why were cats important to ancient Egyptians?

④ ON THE WAY HOME
Thinking It Over

- In the Period Rooms, what objects did you see that we still use today? Have they changed much over time?
- Compare and contrast two different types of art you viewed in the museum.

CAREER FLASH

The following careers relate to the Brooklyn Museum. Do you know what each profession does?

- Archaeologist • Art historian
- Conservator • Museum technician
- Set and exhibit designer

Pick careers to research. What skills and education are needed to pursue these careers?

BROOKLYN NAVY YARD & BLDG 92

63 Flushing Avenue,
Building 92, Brooklyn,
(718) 907-5992

VISIT: bldg92.org

ADMISSION
Building 92: Free

Public Navy Yard tours by bus:
Children *(under 12)*: $15
Adults: $30

HOURS
WED.–SUN. 12 PM–6 PM

HOW TO GET HERE
Subway: Ⓐ Ⓒ Ⓕ Ⓖ

Bus: B48 B57 B62
B67 B69

Ferry:
ferry.nyc/routesand-
schedules/

FOR SPECIAL NEEDS
Wheelchair accessible

SHELLEY REPORTS

Celebrate the rich 200-year history of this site, where real military vessels and battleships were built. You'll also learn what's happening at the Yard now.

- **CHECK OUT THE ANCHOR!** In the lobby of Building 92, see a gigantic anchor from the USS Austin. It weighs about 22,500 pounds.

- **NAVY YARD: PAST, PRESENT, FUTURE** Through ship models, amazing historic objects like a cannon and a ship's steering wheel, and interactive touch screens, discover this naval site's extraordinary past. Located in Building 92.

- **BUS TOURS** Join a guided tour of the Navy Yard's most fascinating sights. Explore a dry dock that's been used since before the Civil War (1861–1865), an old Navy hospital, factories, and more!

MORE INFO: **ShelleysLearningAdventures.com**

SHELLEY'S ACTIVITIES
Fun on the Waterfront!

DID YOU KNOW?

With enough food and water for sailors, modern submarines can stay underwater for up to six months!

1 LET'S GET STARTED

First, visit: bldg92.org

New Places! New Words!

Look up the definition of these words before you go!

- dry dock
- entrepreneur
- industries
- innovator

2 ON THE WAY

Travel Talk

- What is the purpose of having a navy?
- How is living on a boat or submarine different than living on land?
- What are anchors on ships used for? Why are they so large?

3 NOW YOU ARE HERE

Instagram It

Get a pic of yourself posing in front of the giant anchor. See how tiny you look!

Times Change

Spend some time at the touch screen interactive map in Building 92 and learn how the Brooklyn Navy Yard has changed over time!

4 ON THE WAY HOME

Thinking It Over

- What part of living on a ship would you enjoy? What would you dislike?
- Why can boats float even though they are heavy?
- How have naval ships changed throughout history?

CAREER FLASH The following jobs relate to the Brooklyn Navy Yard. Do you know what each profession does?

- **Chief technologist**
- **Director of information technology**
- **Nurse • Sonar technician**
- **Submarine officer**

What skills and education are needed to pursue these careers?

NEARBY ▶ WALK THE BROOKLYN BRIDGE ENTER ON TILLARY STREET *PAGE 148*

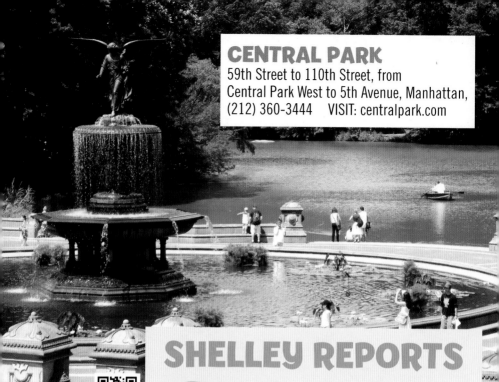

CENTRAL PARK

59th Street to 110th Street, from
Central Park West to 5th Avenue, Manhattan,
(212) 360-3444   VISIT: centralpark.com

SHELLEY REPORTS

Wow! This park has so many beautiful wide-open spaces that are perfect for picnics! There are also 21 playgrounds, rowboats, fishing, ice-skating, a zoo, a cool carousel, and much, much more!

ADMISSION
Free*
Additional activities' prices vary.

HOURS
DAILY 6 AM–1 AM

HOW TO GET HERE
Subway: (A) (B) (C) (D)
(N) (R) (Q) (1) (2) (3)
(4) (5) (6)

Bus: M1 M2 M3 M4
M10 M20 M57 M66
M72 M79 M86 M96
M106 M116 Q32

FOR SPECIAL NEEDS
lslearn.info/nycparks

- **ZOO AND PLAYGROUNDS** Visit the animals and explore Central Park's many playgrounds! There are giant rocks and pyramids for climbing, granite slides, an Alice in Wonderland spray fountain, and more!

- **KIDS' DISCOVERY KITS** Stop by a park visitor center to borrow a backpack filled with a free Discovery Journal, binoculars, a field guide, and colored pencils!

- **HARLEM MEER** Borrow fishing poles from the nearby Discovery Center and try your hand at catch-and-release fishing (free bait also provided).

- **LOEB BOATHOUSE** From April to October, rent a rowboat or gondola for an afternoon on the water!

MORE INFO: **ShelleysLearningAdventures.com**

SHELLEY'S ACTIVITIES
Nature in Manhattan

DID YOU KNOW?

Central Park was once filled with grazing sheep. That's how the Sheep Meadow got its name!

3 NOW YOU ARE HERE

Music To Your Ears
Find the Delacorte Music Clock to enjoy hearing popular nursery rhymes that play every half hour.

Field Day!
At the North Meadow Recreation Center, borrow a free field day kit with supplies to play Frisbee, catch, or jump rope!

1 LET'S GET STARTED

First, visit: centralpark.com

New Places! New Words!
Look up the definition of these words before you go!

- arch
- bedrock
- conservancy
- reservoir

2 ON THE WAY

Travel Talk
- Why are parks important to people who live in cities?
- How is Central Park similar to a park near your home? How is it different?
- What are some activities you can do in a park that are hard to do elsewhere in the city?

4 ON THE WAY HOME

Thinking It Over
- Why do you think a lot of movies are filmed in Central Park?
- What activities would you recommend to someone exploring the park for the first time?

CAREER FLASH

The following careers relate to Central Park. Do you know what each type of profession does?

- Construction manager
- Horticulturist
- Landscape architect
- Urban park manager

Pick careers to research. What skills and education are needed to pursue these careers?

NEARBY ▶ AMERICAN MUSEUM OF NATURAL HISTORY 79TH STREET & CENTRAL PARK WEST *PAGE 4*
METROPOLITAN MUSEUM OF ART 1000 5TH AVENUE *PAGE 64*

21

CHILDREN'S MUSEUM OF MANHATTAN

212 W. 83rd Street Manhattan, (212) 721-1223   VISIT: cmom.org

ADMISSION

Children *(under 1)*: Free
General Admission: $14
Seniors *(65+)*: $11

HOURS

TUES.–FRI.
10 AM.–5 PM
SAT. 10 AM–7 PM
SUN. 10 AM–5 PM
MON. *(summer)*
10 AM-5PM

HOW TO GET HERE

Subway: **B C 1**

Bus: M7 M10 M11
M104 M79 M86

FOR SPECIAL NEEDS

lslearn.info/cmom

SHELLEY REPORTS

Wow! Five fabulous floors of interactive exhibits! There are also more than 80 workshops, classes, and performances each week. This museum is truly magical for young children.

- **LET'S DANCE!** Leap, boogie, and groove. This exhibit celebrates the joy of dance.

- **EATSLEEPPLAY™** Through a variety of exciting games and activities, discover how eating right and moving your body can be lots of fun!

- **DYNAMIC H₂O** During warm weather, step outside to cool off with water-based play. Learn the importance of water in our lives through wet and wild activities!

- **PLAYWORKS™** Find out how fun it is to learn by playing. Meet a giant talking dragon that "eats" letters!

MORE INFO: **ShelleysLearningAdventures.com**

SHELLEY'S ACTIVITIES
A Museum of Fun!

DID YOU KNOW?

Your heart is your body's hardest-working muscle. It beats around 100,000 times per day!

① LET'S GET STARTED

First, visit: cmom.org

New Places! New Words!

Look up the definition of these words before you go!

- choreography
- engineer
- nutrients
- obesity

② ON THE WAY
Travel Talk

- What's your favorite type of exercise? Why do you like it?
- Why do you think it is important to get a good night's sleep?

③ NOW YOU ARE HERE
Dance Show!

In the Let's Dance! area, take a vlog of yourself doing your best dance move ever!

Art Lab

In the PlayWorks™ exhibit, check out the Art Lab activity! From painting to creating sun catchers, themed activities change regularly!

④ ON THE WAY HOME
Thinking It Over

- What songs make you want to dance?
- Describe three things you learned from exploring the Museum.
- How did you use your senses of touch, hearing, and sight at the Museum?

CAREER FLASH

The following careers relate to the Children's Museum of Manhattan. Do you know what each profession does?

- Cultural educator
- Dance therapist
- Party planner
- School programs educator

What skills and education are needed to pursue these careers?

NEARBY ▶ AMERICAN MUSEUM OF NATURAL HISTORY 79TH STREET & CENTRAL PARK WEST *PAGE 4*
CENTRAL PARK ENTER ON 81ST STREET *PAGE 20*

CHILDREN'S MUSEUM OF THE ARTS

103 Charlton Street, Manhattan, (212) 274-0986   VISIT: cmany.org

SHELLEY REPORTS

From the Clay Bar to the Sound Booth, there are lots of hands-on, creative art activities where you don't just view the art, you make it!

ADMISSION
Children *(under 1)*: Free
General Admission: $12
Seniors *(65+)*: Pay what you wish.

HOURS
MON. 12 PM–5 PM
THUR.–FRI. 12 PM–6 PM
SAT.–SUN. 10 AM–5 PM

HOW TO GET HERE
Subway: Ⓐ Ⓑ Ⓒ
Ⓓ Ⓔ Ⓕ Ⓜ ①
Bus: M20 M21

FOR SPECIAL NEEDS
lslearn.info/cmoa

- **CLAY BAR** Sculpt a purple unicorn, a growling tiger, or an alien—whatever fabulous creature you imagine, teaching artists help you create it!

- **SOUND BOOTH** Use digital instruments to mix your own tune, record yourself singing, and more! Open on Thursdays, Saturdays, and Sundays.

- **MEDIA LAB** Changing activities include creating animated movies, editing film scenes, and exploring the art of digital photography.

- **FINE ARTS STUDIO** Use glitter, yarn, fabric, wire, or paint to create imaginative arts and crafts, such as portraits, jewelry, stamps, and magnets! Themed activities change regularly.

MORE INFO: **ShelleysLearningAdventures.com**

SHELLEY'S ACTIVITIES
Take Part in Art!

DID YOU KNOW?

Micro painters can create amazing works of art, including portraits and landscapes, on a single grain of rice.

3 NOW YOU ARE HERE
Insta-Story!
Build a clay animal, then tell a story on Instagram about the creature's adventures!

Paint a Portrait!
Create a self-portrait using paint or other art supplies at the Fine Arts Studio.

1 LET'S GET STARTED
First, visit: cmany.org

New Places! New Words!
Look up the definition of these words before you go!

- innovation
- masterpiece
- media
- portrait

4 ON THE WAY HOME
Thinking It Over

- Compare and contrast the different types of materials you used to create your art.
- What different types of art do you like? Why?
- Why have people throughout history created art?

2 ON THE WAY
Travel Talk

- Where might artists get ideas for their creations?
- What kinds of emotions can art make you feel?
- Think about what type of art you might create. What materials will you need?

CAREER FLASH The following careers relate to the Children's Museum of the Arts. Do you know what each profession does?

- **Art therapist**
- **Audio engineer**
- **Filmmaking instructor**
- **Sound engineer**

Pick careers to research. What skills and education are needed to pursue these careers?

NEARBY → **HUDSON RIVER PARK** ENTER ON HOUSTON STREET *PAGE 50*
NEW YORK CITY FIRE MUSEUM 278 SPRING STREET *PAGE 90*

CITY ISLAND

City Island, Bronx, (718) 885-9100   VISIT: cityislandchamber.org

ADMISSION
Free*
*Additional activities' prices vary.

HOW TO GET HERE
Subway: 6

From Manhattan, Brooklyn, or Queens: take the #6 train north to Pelham Bay Park, then transfer to the Bx29 City Island bus.

Bus: Bx29 BxM8

SHELLEY REPORTS

Ahoy, sailor! This salty island feels like a quaint New England fishing village with spectacular water views, seafood restaurants, and boats everywhere you turn!

- **CITY ISLAND NAUTICAL MUSEUM** Discover wooden boats, military vessels, and more. Open weekends during warmer months.

- **GO FISHING** Fishing boats with captains are available to take you out to Long Island Sound. Also available are small motor boats for rent from Jack's Bait and Tackle for fishing.

- **CATCH OF THE DAY** Seafood lovers can go overboard with a wide selection of fresh seafood restaurants.

SHELLEY'S ACTIVITIES
New England in the Bronx!

People who were born and raised on City Island are nicknamed "clam diggers."

1 LET'S GET STARTED

First, visit:
cityislandchamber.org

New Places! New Words!
Look up the definition of these words before you go!

- bait
- maritime
- nautical
- schooner
- species

2 ON THE WAY
Travel Talk

- What different types of species live in and around Long Island Sound?
- How is the ocean important to communities like City Island?

3 NOW YOU ARE HERE
Take a Walk
Stroll down Horton, William, Belden, Minneford, or King streets to admire the ornate Victorian homes!

Cool It
On a hot day, take a dash through the water jets at the playground in Ambrosini Field!

4 ON THE WAY HOME
Thinking It Over

- How are Victorian homes different from houses built today?
- How do wildlife and people interact with each other in places like City Island?
- Why might someone want to live on City Island instead of in Manhattan?

CAREER FLASH The following careers relate to City Island. Do you know what each profession does?

- Antique-shop owner
- Chef
- Commercial fisherman
- Shipwright

Pick careers to research. What skills and education are needed to pursue these careers?

BRONX

FREE

SHELLEY REPORTS

ADMISSION
Free

HOURS
Check website for lecture times.

HOW TO GET HERE
Subway: ①

Bus: M4 M5 M11
M60 M104

Enter the main campus at 116th Street and Broadway, then proceed northeast to Pupin Hall.

FOR SPECIAL NEEDS
Lectures wheelchair accessible, but observations on the roof are not.

> Truly out of this world! Meet real astronomers and use powerful rooftop telescopes to gaze at the stars far, far above.

- **LECTURE SERIES** Every other Friday during the school year, meet astronomers who share info about space, from constellations to life on other planets. It's truly spectacular!

- **STARGAZING** At many events, astronomers bring their high-tech telescopes outside to the roof, so you can get a close-up look at the stars and moon above. It'll wow you! Check the website the day of a lecture to confirm whether stargazing will be possible.

- **AMATEUR ASTRONOMERS ASSOCIATION OF NEW YORK** Check out this organization's website for more incredible lectures and stargazing events. Visit aaa.org to learn more.

MORE INFO: **ShelleysLearningAdventures.com**

SHELLEY'S ACTIVITIES
Gaze at the Wonders of Space!

DID YOU KNOW?

About 1.3 million Earths could fit inside the sun!

① LET'S GET STARTED

First, visit: outreach.astro.columbia.edu

New Places! New Words!

Look up the definition of these words before you go!

- astronomer
- constellation
- meteor
- telescope

② ON THE WAY
Travel Talk

- What makes the Earth special compared to other planets in our solar system?
- How many of the planets can you name?
- Would you rather live in outer space or underwater? Why?

③ NOW YOU ARE HERE
Ask an Expert

After the lecture, ask the astronomer a question about something they shared!

Cool Constellations

Ask the astronomer guides to point out constellations. See how many you can find!

④ ON THE WAY HOME
Thinking It Over

- Would you want to be an astronaut? Why or why not?
- If you could travel to any planet in outer space, where would you go?
- Why do you think it's important for people to study outer space?

CAREER FLASH

The following careers relate to astronomy. Do you know what each profession does?

- Aerospace engineer
- Astronaut
- NASA programmer
- Observatory scientist
- Science teacher

Pick careers to research. What skills and education are needed to pursue these careers?

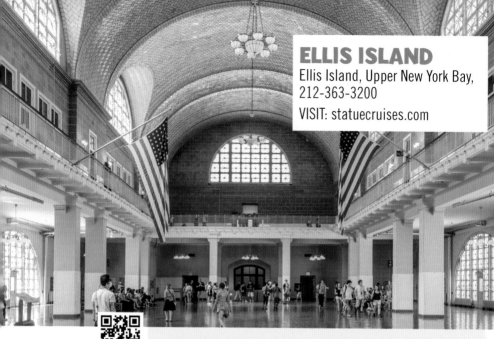

ELLIS ISLAND
Ellis Island, Upper New York Bay,
212-363-3200
VISIT: statuecruises.com

ADMISSION*
Children *(under 4)*: Free
Children *(4–12)*: $9
Adults: $18.50
Seniors *(62+)*: $14
Includes admission to Ellis Island and Liberty Island grounds.

HOURS
Manhattan Ferry:
DAILY DEPARTURES
8:30 AM–5 PM

HOW TO GET HERE
Manhattan Ferry
(Castle Clinton at Battery Park):
Subway:
R W 1 4 5
Bus: M1 M6 M15

FOR SPECIAL NEEDS
lslearn.info/ellis

SHELLEY REPORTS

Imagine leaving your home and sailing on a crowded ship to a new and strange land. That's what millions of Americans did before they arrived as new immigrants at Ellis Island.

- **PARK RANGER TOUR** At the information booth, join a free tour to learn about immigrants' journeys to America. It's fascinating!

- **BAGGAGE ROOM** See century-old luggage and imagine being an immigrant arriving in this room! While you're there, check out the glowing World Migration Globe—it's impossible to miss!

- **GREAT HALL** This giant room was often crowded and overwhelming for new arrivals.

- **TREASURES FROM HOME** See the prized possessions like handmade linens and toys that immigrants brought to the US.

SHELLEY'S ACTIVITIES
Island of Hope

DID YOU KNOW?

Many immigrants coming to the US through Ellis Island could only bring what they could carry in a small bag or suitcase.

① LET'S GET STARTED

First, visit: statuecruises.com

New Places! New Words!

Look up the definition of these words before you go!

- citizenship
- immigrant
- manifest
- steerage

② ON THE WAY
Travel Talk

- Why might someone leave their home country to move to the US?
- What challenges do immigrants often face when coming to the US?
- What are some things an immigrant might need to learn before traveling to a different country?

③ NOW YOU ARE HERE
All Ears!

Ask for the family-friendly audio tour and listen as it guides you through the fascinating museum at Ellis Island.

Be an Ellis Kid

Imagine you are an immigrant at Ellis Island. Share your pretend experience with your family.

④ ON THE WAY HOME
Thinking It Over

- How do you think immigrants felt when first landing at Ellis Island?
- If you had to leave home and could only bring what fit in one backpack, what would you bring?
- Why was Ellis Island known as the "Isle of Hope"?

 CAREER FLASH The following careers relate to Ellis Island and immigration. Do you know what each profession does?

- Family genealogist
- Immigrant physician
- Immigration customs agent
- Immigration lawyer

What skills and education are needed to pursue these careers?

NEARBY → SKYSCRAPER MUSEUM 39 BATTERY PLACE *PAGE 116*
STATUE OF LIBERTY LIBERTY ISLAND *PAGE 126*

EL MUSEO DEL BARRIO

1230 5th Avenue, Manhattan, (212) 831-7272

VISIT: elmuseo.org

A MUSEUM IS A SCHOOL: THE ARTIST LEARNS TO COMMUNICATE. THE PUBLIC LEARNS TO MAKE CON...

SHELLEY REPORTS

This little gem of a museum shines a light on the history, culture, and art of Latin America and the Caribbean, while highlighting the many contributions of Latino culture to the US.

ADMISSION

Children *(under 12)*: Free
Students: $5
Adults: $9
Seniors: $5

HOURS

Visit website to view up-to-date museum hours.

HOW TO GET HERE

Subway: ② ③ ⑥

Bus: M1 M2 M3 M4

FOR SPECIAL NEEDS

lslearn.info/elmuseob

- **TAÍNO/PRE-COLUMBIAN ARTIFACTS** Learn about myths, ceremonies, and life in Puerto Rico and the Dominican Republic long ago!

- **SUPER *SÁBADO*** On the third Saturday each month, enjoy storytelling, art workshops, and exciting Latin-themed music and entertainment for children!

- **CONTEMPORARY ART** Admire bright paintings, photography, videos, and mixed-media artwork by modern Latino artists. Gorgeous!

- **POPULAR TRADITIONS** Experience the unique holidays that different Latin Americans celebrate!

SHELLEY'S ACTIVITIES
Latino Culture & Arts Come Alive!

DID YOU KNOW?

During *El Día de los Muertos*, bright-yellow marigold flowers represent life and hope.

① LET'S GET STARTED

First, visit: elmuseo.org

New Places! New Words!

Look up the definition of these words before you go!

- *barrio*
- *El Día de los Muertos*
- diaspora
- heritage

② ON THE WAY
Travel Talk

- What traditions or holidays does your family observe to celebrate your heritage?
- How can you learn about cultures by looking at works of art?
- What are some ways you can research how your ancestors, grandparents, or parents came to the US?

③ NOW YOU ARE HERE
Instagram Review

Post photos on Instagram of your favorite art pieces on display, along with a short review of the museum!

Masked Meanings

Check out the collection of Mexican and Guatemalan masks. Pick your favorite and ponder the meaning behind its details.

④ ON THE WAY HOME
Thinking It Over

- Why do some traditions from long ago survive today, while others don't?
- Why is it important to preserve artifacts from the past?

CAREER FLASH

The following careers relate to El Museo del Barrio. Do you know what each profession does?

- **Art preservationist**
- **Audio engineer**
- **Community outreach specialist**
- **Santero artist**
- **Social media coordinator**

Pick careers to research. What skills and education are needed to pursue these careers?

FDNY FIRE ZONE
Rockefeller Center, 34 W. 51st
Street, Manhattan, (212) 698-4520
VISIT: fdnysmart.org/firezone

SHELLEY REPORTS

GENERAL ADMISSION
Free

**FIRE SAFETY
PRESENTATION**
Children and Adults: $6
Seniors *(60+)*: $2
Only suitable for ages 5+

HOURS
MON.-SAT. 9 AM–7 PM
SUN. 11 AM–5 PM

HOW TO GET HERE
Subway: Ⓑ Ⓓ Ⓕ Ⓜ
Ⓝ Ⓠ Ⓡ ① ⑥

Bus: M1 M2 M3 M4
M5 M7 M50

FOR SPECIAL NEEDS
The FDNY Fire Zone
is fully wheelchair
accessible.

Would you know what to do if a fire
started in your house? At the FDNY
Fire Zone, retired firefighters use a
cool interactive exhibit to show you
how to be safe.

- **BE ONE OF NEW YORK'S BRAVEST** Get ready! Hop
  aboard a real fire truck, sit in the driver's seat, and give
  the steering wheel a spin. Fun!

- **HOW TO SURVIVE** Through special effects, sound,
  lighting, and a video presentation, learn about common
  fire hazards and lifesaving tips for escaping a fire.

- **SMOKY HALLWAY** Can you carefully crawl through
  a "smoke-filled" corridor to make it to safety? This
  exercise teaches the importance of fire escape plans.

- **HOT DOOR** With help from firefighter instructors,
  discover how touching a door before opening it may
  protect you from a fire. This is important stuff!

MORE INFO: **ShelleysLearningAdventures.com**

SHELLEY'S ACTIVITIES
Fire Safety!

DID YOU KNOW?

Cooking is the leading cause of home fires and home fire injuries.

① LET'S GET STARTED

First, visit:
fdnysmart.org/firezone

New Places! New Words!

Look up the definition of these words before you go!

- escape
- emergency
- fire hydrant
- hazard
- oxygen

② ON THE WAY
Travel Talk

- Does your family have a fire emergency plan for your home?
- Besides candles, what are some other possible fire hazards in your house?
- How do you call for help in an emergency? When is it okay to call emergency services? When is it not?

③ NOW YOU ARE HERE
Insta-Firefighter

Put on a firefighter's coat and hop in the fire truck for a fun, Instagram-worthy photo!

So Many Badges!

Compare and contrast the different fire badges on the wall. Which is your favorite? Why?

④ ON THE WAY HOME
Thinking It Over

- How often should your family test their smoke alarms?
- What should you do if your clothes catch on fire?
- Create a fire safety plan for your home and family.

CAREER FLASH

The following careers relate to the FDNY Fire Zone. Do you know what each profession does?

- Director of social media • EMT
- Firefighter • Fire protection engineer
- Fire safety educator

Pick careers to research. What skills and education are needed to pursue these careers?

NEARBY ➡ SCIENCE THEATER COMPANY, THE PLAYROOM THEATER 151 W. 46TH STREET *PAGE 114*
THE TOUR AT NBC STUDIOS 30 ROCKEFELLER PLAZA *PAGE 142*

FISHING IN SHEEPSHEAD BAY

Marilyn Jean IV:
2200 Emmons Avenue,
Brooklyn, (917) 650-3212
VISIT: mj2fishing.com

Sea Queen VII:
2250 Emmons Avenue,
Brooklyn, (917) 642-0265
VISIT: seaqueenvii.com

Capt. Dave III:
2498 Emmons Avenue,
Brooklyn, (347) 699-3651
VISIT: captdaveonline.com

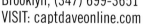

ADMISSION/HOURS
Fishing boat times and rates vary by company. Check websites for times and cost.

HOW TO GET HERE
Subway: B Q

Bus: B4

FOR SPECIAL NEEDS
Call fishing boat to discuss accessibility.

SHELLEY REPORTS

A fishing village in Brooklyn? Take a stroll down Emmons Avenue in Sheepshead Bay and you'll find many fishing boats to take you out on a great fishing adventure!

- **PICK YOUR TRIP!** From night trips to day trips, every outing is different, and can last a half or full day. Check the companies' websites and pick one that floats your boat!

- **WHAT TO BRING** Dress in layers, bring some snacks, and put on lots of sunscreen! As for the rods, tackle, bait, and other fishing supplies, most companies provide them for free or a small charge.

- **TIME TO EAT** Before or after your fishing adventure, enjoy a meal on Emmons Avenue.

MORE INFO: **ShelleysLearningAdventures.com**

SHELLEY'S ACTIVITIES
Catch a Big Fish in Brooklyn!

DID YOU KNOW?

Striped bass don't have eyelids! When the sun is out, they swim into deeper water to avoid sunlight.

① LET'S GET STARTED

First, visit: mj2fishing.com, seaqueenvii.com, or captdaveonline.com

New Places! New Words!

Look up the definition of these words before you go!

- angling
- bait
- barb
- tackle

② ON THE WAY
Travel Talk

- What is the purpose of catch-and-release fishing?
- Other than a fishing rod, what other tools do people use to catch fish?
- Why are some fishing trips scheduled for nighttime instead of daytime?

③ NOW YOU ARE HERE
Pic-collage!

Snap photos of your fishing adventure—and any fish you catch! Use a photo app to make a collage of your day.

Fishy Tips

Ask the captain or boat staff for tips on catching fish, and about their most fun adventures out at sea!

④ ON THE WAY HOME
Thinking It Over

- Why are there many different types of bait?
- What tools have helped people become better at catching fish?
- Why are there laws about the types and number of fish you can catch?

CAREER FLASH The following careers relate to fishing at Sheepshead Bay. Do you know what each profession does?

- Boat mate
- Fish biologist
- Fishing boat captain
- Marine mechanic
- Seafood broker

Pick careers to research. What skills and education are needed to pursue these careers?

GAZILLION BUBBLE SHOW
New World Stages,
340 W. 50th Street, Manhattan,
(212) 239-6200

VISIT: gazillionbubbleshow.com

SHELLEY REPORTS

Bubbles, bubbles everywhere, even bubbles in the shape of a square! This show is so cool that it includes the creation of some of the world's largest bubbles!

ADMISSION
Ticket prices start at $59. Check website to view available seats and to purchase tickets.

SHOWTIMES
FRI. 7 PM
SAT. 11 AM, 2 PM, 4:30 PM
SUN. 12 PM, 3 PM

HOW TO GET HERE
Subway: B C D E F M N Q R 1

Bus: M11 M20 M50 M104

FOR SPECIAL NEEDS
Wheelchair accessible

- **BUBBLE SHOW** You'll ask "How'd they do that?" at every moment of this spectacular performance. Bubbles in all shapes and sizes—plus a bubble blizzard—will amaze you!

- **VOLUNTEER** Raise a hand to be picked to go on stage! If chosen, you may find yourself standing inside of a gigantic bubble. So cool!

- **LASER LIGHTS** The bubbles shimmer and dazzle throughout the show with the addition of colorful lasers. It's so very special.

- **BUBBLE PHOTO** Before or after the performance, purchase a souvenir picture of yourself inside a huge bubble. It's a memento of an unforgettable show!

SHELLEY'S ACTIVITIES
Bubbles! Bubbles! Everywhere!

DID YOU KNOW?

Bubbles can't form in outer space! Air pressure creates a bubble's shape, but there is no air in space!

① LET'S GET STARTED

First, visit:
gazillionbubbleshow.com

New Places! New Words!

Look up the definition of these words before you go!

- blizzard
- gazillion
- laser
- shimmer

② ON THE WAY
Travel Talk

- How are bubbles made? What materials and equipment are needed?

- What is stronger: a bubble made from soap or a bubble made from gum? Why?

- Why are some bubbles able to float in the air before they pop?

③ NOW YOU ARE HERE
Bubble Records

Can you research which Guinness World Records are about bubbles?

Share the Fun!

After the show ends, create an Instagram story to share your favorite part of the bubble show with friends.

④ ON THE WAY HOME
Thinking It Over

- Why do rainbow colors appear on some bubbles?

- How was the performer able to create the giant bubbles without popping them?

- Can you imagine what it's like to perform on stage? Would you like to be a performer?

CAREER FLASH The following careers relate to the Gazillion Bubble Show. Do you know what each profession does?

- Light board operator
- Social media coordinator
- Sound technician • Stage performer

Pick careers to research. What skills and education are needed to pursue these careers?

NEARBY → FDNY FIRE ZONE ROCKEFELLER CENTER, 34 W. 51ST STREET *PAGE 34*
GULLIVER'S GATE 216 W. 44TH STREET *PAGE 44*

GOVERNORS ISLAND
Manhattan Ferry: 10 South Street, Manhattan,
(212) 440-2200   VISIT: govisland.com

FERRY ADMISSION*
Children *(under 13)*: Free
Adults *(13+)*: $3
Seniors *(65+)*: $1
*Additional activities'
prices vary.*

HOURS
May 1–Oct. 31
MON.–FRI. 10 AM–6 PM
FRI. *(May 26–Sep. 14)*
10 AM–9 PM
SAT.–SUN. 10 AM–7 PM

HOW TO GET HERE
**Subway to Manhattan
ferry***: R 1 4 5

**Bus to Manhattan
ferry***: M9 M15
*Manhattan ferry runs
every day. Free on Sat.
and Sun. until 11:30 AM.
Ferries from Brooklyn also.*

FOR SPECIAL NEEDS
lslearn.info/govisland

SHELLEY REPORTS

Here's a getaway island that even a pirate would love! There's ziplining and climbing walls, forts and castles, huge hammocks and mini golf, bike riding, and so many other treasures.

- **BIKING** Quadricycle, tandem bikes, and beach cruisers are all available to rent—or bring your own bike and have a blast exploring seven miles of car-free trails!

- **Play:groundNYC** Use nails, hammers, wood, fabrics, and other recycled materials to build and create to your heart's content!

- **COMPOST LEARNING CENTER** Discover how thousands of pounds of food scraps are composted to become soil and reused. Remarkable! And you may also meet goats and chickens! (Open weekends.)

- **TEACHING GARDEN** Explore this urban garden with more than 20 vegetable beds, an outdoor kitchen, and more! (Open weekends.)

MORE INFO: **ShelleysLearningAdventures.com**

SHELLEY'S ACTIVITIES
Active Island Adventures!

DID YOU KNOW?

In 1909, Wilbur Wright took off from Governors Island, making the first-ever flight over water!

① LET'S GET STARTED

First, visit: govisland.com

New Places! New Words!

Look up the definition of these words before you go!

- composting
- fort
- quadracycle
- sentinel
- zipline

② ON THE WAY
Travel Talk

- How might a playground designer consider angles and distances when designing a maze or playground?
- Where do you think the fruits and vegetables you eat are grown? In NYC, or elsewhere?

③ NOW YOU ARE HERE
Chill Out

Take a selfie stretching out on a grassy field. But make sure you don't fall asleep!

Play Time!

At the Hammock Grove Play Area and adjacent Liggett Terrace, climb, swing, and—on warmer days—run through the water jets!

④ ON THE WAY HOME
Thinking It Over

- If you designed your own island, what would it include?
- Why was Fort Jay built? What purpose did it serve?

CAREER FLASH

The following careers relate to Governors Island. Do you know what each profession does?

- Director of event programming
- Environmental educator
- Park ranger • Playground architect
- Urban farmer

Pick careers to research. What skills and education are needed to pursue these careers?

NEARBY ➤ NATIONAL MUSEUM OF THE AMERICAN INDIAN ONE BOWLING GREEN *PAGE 82*
SKYSCRAPER MUSEUM 39 BATTERY PLACE *PAGE 116*

GRAND CENTRAL TERMINAL
89 E. 42nd Street, Manhattan, (212) 340-2583
VISIT: grandcentralterminal.com

ADMISSION
Free

AUDIO TOURS
$7–$9
Visit website for more info.

HOURS
DAILY 5:30 AM–2 AM

HOW TO GET HERE
Subway:

Bus: M1 M2 M3 M4 M42 M101 M102 M103 Q32

Train: MTA Metro-North Railroad

FOR SPECIAL NEEDS
Wheelchair accessible

SHELLEY REPORTS

This world-famous station transports more than 750,000 commuters each day! It's a dazzling architectural wonder!

- **GRAND CENTRAL FACADE** On 42nd Street outside Grand Central, spot the colorful clock up above! Also look for the statues of Hercules, Mercury, and Minerva!

- **MAIN CONCOURSE** Grand Central's ceiling includes astrological symbols and mythical creatures that span the dome, which is painted like a bright blue sky! And don't forget to gaze at the giant train schedule up above the fare windows! Wow!

- **MEET YOU AT THE CLOCK** Every day, thousands of visitors meet at the four-sided brass clock on top of the terminal's info booth. The iconic clock is worth more than $20 million!

MORE INFO: **ShelleysLearningAdventures.com**

SHELLEY'S ACTIVITIES
NYC's Grandest Station!

DID YOU KNOW?

Look up! The constellations on Grand Central's domed ceiling were painted backwards. No one knows if it was done on purpose!

① LET'S GET STARTED

First, visit: grandcentralterminal.com

New Places! New Words!

Look up the definition of these words before you go!

- architecture
- astrology
- beaux arts
- constellation
- terminal

② ON THE WAY
Travel Talk

- Why is it important to keep historic buildings like Grand Central Terminal from being torn down?
- Why are so many of NYC's train tracks and subways built underground?

③ NOW YOU ARE HERE
Can You Spot It?

Look at the ceiling—can you spot the dirty tile by the crab constellation? That's how the ceiling looked before it was cleaned!

Whispering Gallery

Press your ear to the tiled wall of the arches near GCT's Oyster Bar to hear conversations from across the hall! It sure is an acoustic oddity!

④ ON THE WAY HOME
Thinking It Over

- How does a train station impact where a city's residents live, work, and travel?
- Why do so many people enjoy the architectural beauty of Grand Central Terminal?

CAREER FLASH The following careers relate to Grand Central Terminal. Do you know what each profession does?

- Conductor
- Locomotive engineer
- Mural restoration artist
- Retail consultant
- Urban planner

What skills and education are needed to pursue these careers?

NEARBY **NY PUBLIC LIBRARY & LIBRARY WAY** 5TH AVENUE & 42ND STREET *PAGE 96*
UNITED NATIONS 405 E. 42ND STREET *PAGE 144*

GULLIVER'S GATE

216 W. 44th Street, Manhattan,
(212) 235-2016
VISIT: gulliversgate.com

ADMISSION

Children *(under 6)*: Free
Children *(6–12)*: $27
Adults *(13–64)*: $36
Seniors *(65+)*: $27

HOURS

DAILY 10 AM–8 PM

HOW TO GET HERE

Subway: Ⓐ Ⓑ Ⓒ Ⓓ
Ⓔ Ⓕ Ⓜ Ⓝ Ⓠ Ⓡ
Ⓢ Ⓦ ① ② ③ ⑦

Bus: M7 M20 M104

FOR SPECIAL NEEDS

Wheelchair accessible

SHELLEY REPORTS

> Take a walk around the world in this dazzling miniature exhibit that is almost the size of one city block!

- **WORLD EXHIBITS** From Peru's ancient city of Machu Picchu, to India's gorgeous Taj Mahal, to Europe's famed Matterhorn mountain, marvel at our extraordinary world—in miniature!

- **NYC EXHIBIT** Spot everything from your favorite pizzeria to marvelous New York landmarks as you get lost in this incredible miniature version of the city. It's spectacular!

- **USE A MAGIC KEY** Get a "magic key" to bring special miniatures to life—make a helicopter fly, send skiers down a mountain, and more!

SHELLEY'S ACTIVITIES
It's a Small World!

DID YOU KNOW?

In the book *Gulliver's Travels*, Gulliver experiences both giants and tiny humans during his travels. The Lilliputians were only 6 inches tall.

1 LET'S GET STARTED

First, visit: gulliversgate.com.

New Places! New Words!

Look up the definition of these words before you go!

- landmark
- Lilliputian
- miniature
- Taj Mahal

2 ON THE WAY
Travel Talk

- What does it mean to shrink things down "to scale"?

- Where would you go if you could take a vacation anywhere in the world?

- Imagine being the size of an ant. Compare and contrast it with your life today.

3 NOW YOU ARE HERE
Can You Find It?

In NYC, find the *Fearless Girl* statue. What other landmarks can you spot?

#GulliversGate!

Add the tag #GulliversGate to your photos on social media to share them with the museum!

4 ON THE WAY HOME
Thinking It Over

- How do you think model builders study a location before building it in miniature?

- What miniature details most impressed you?

- After looking at the miniatures, which country or place do you want to learn more about?

CAREER FLASH The following careers relate to Gulliver's Gate. Do you know what each profession does?

- **Chief technology officer**
- **Content producer**
- **Control room operator**
- **Mechanical engineer**
- **Social media manager**

What skills and education are needed to pursue these careers?

NEARBY ➤ **NATIONAL GEOGRAPHIC ENCOUNTER: OCEAN ODYSSEY** 226 W. 44TH STREET *PAGE 78*
THE NEW VICTORY THEATER 209 W. 42ND STREET *PAGE 140*

45

HISTORIC AIRCRAFT RESTORATION PROJECT (HARP)

Gateway National Recreation Area, Floyd Bennett Field,
50 Aviation Road, Brooklyn, (718) 338-3799

VISIT: nps.gov/gate/getinvolved/supportyourpark/the-angels-of-harp.htm

ADMISSION
Free

HOURS
TUES., THUR., SAT.
9 AM–3 PM

RANGER-GUIDED TOURS
SUN. 2 PM–4 PM

HOW TO GET HERE
Subway: A S 2 5

Bus: Q35

FOR SPECIAL NEEDS
Hangar and visitor's
center are wheelchair
accessible.

SHELLEY REPORTS

Wow, this place is a real NYC hidden gem! It's a spectacular collection of more than 10 incredible airplanes from just about every era of aviation history!

- **HANGAR B** From cargo freighters, to sea planes, to a full-scale model of the Wright Brothers' flyer, get up close to some famous historical aircraft. This is amazing!

- **RYAN VISITOR CENTER** Don't miss the children's activity area to design your own gliding paper airplanes, sit in a mock cockpit, "fly" a mini-plane, and more terrific aviation-themed fun!

- **TALK TO A VOLUNTEER** Volunteers at HARP range from military veterans, to former commercial pilots, to people who just love everything about airplanes! Be sure to ask them questions—they'll share their knowledge and talk about planes that are being restored!

MORE INFO: **ShelleysLearningAdventures.com**

SHELLEY'S ACTIVITIES
History Flies in Brooklyn!

DID YOU KNOW?

The Tuskegee Airmen were the first African American pilots in the U.S. Air Force and served during World War II. In 2007 they were awarded the Congressional Medal of Honor for their bravery.

③ NOW YOU ARE HERE
What's the History?

At Hangar B, find a plane that looks cool or unusual. Ask a volunteer to tell you about it!

Best Flyer

At the Ryan Visitor Center, make a few different paper airplanes and see which one flies the farthest!

① LET'S GET STARTED

First, visit: nps.gov/gate/getinvolved/supportyourpark/the-angels-of-harp.htm

New Places! New Words!

Look up the definition of these words before you go!

- biplane
- cockpit
- hangar
- restoration
- solo

② ON THE WAY
Travel Talk

- Before airplanes, how did people travel long distances?
- When did the first airplane take flight?
- Why do people restore old airplanes, even if the planes don't fly anymore?

④ ON THE WAY HOME
Thinking It Over

- Compare and contrast military jets with the planes we use to travel.
- How many types of aircraft can you name? How do they differ?
- How did airplanes change the way people live, travel, and work around the world?

CAREER FLASH

The following careers relate to HARP. Do you know what each profession does?

- Aircraft electrical installer
- Aviation historian
- Flight attendant
- National park ranger
- Pilot

Pick careers to research. What skills and education are needed to pursue these careers?

NEARBY ➤ WHALE WATCHING WITH AMERICAN PRINCESS CRUISES RIIS LANDING *PAGE 150*

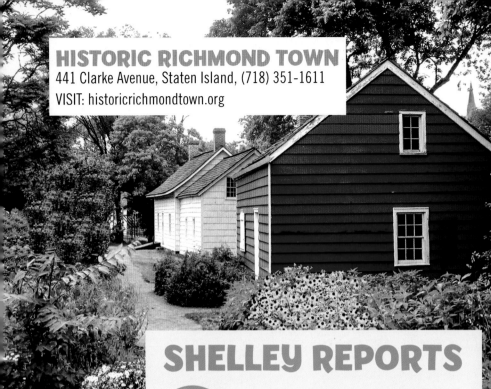

HISTORIC RICHMOND TOWN
441 Clarke Avenue, Staten Island, (718) 351-1611
VISIT: historicrichmondtown.org

ADMISSION
Adults: $8
Children *(0–3)*: Free
Children *(4–11)*: $5,
Children *(12–17)*: $6
Seniors *(62+)*: $6
Students: $6

HOURS
WED.–SUN. 1 PM–5 PM

HOW TO GET HERE
Ferry:
Staten Island Ferry
Bus: S53 S74

FOR SPECIAL NEEDS
lslearn.info/histrich

SHELLEY REPORTS

This is real time travel on Staten Island! There are over 30 historic buildings and more than 130,000 artifacts about life in America from the mid-1600s to today.

- **DAILY GUIDED TOURS** With different tours each day, these experiences are a blast from the past. Come stroll Richmond Town and imagine life hundreds of years ago!

- **BUILDING THE AMERICAN DREAM** On Sundays, this unique artisan's tour lets you step into places like the tinsmith's shop and the basket maker's house. Learn the skills people used to build cities and towns across America.

- **GENERAL STORE** From lamps to soap to spices, tour this shop to see the types of products villagers in the 1800s needed. It's a fascinating glimpse into daily life long ago!

MORE INFO: **ShelleysLearningAdventures.com**

SHELLEY'S ACTIVITIES
History Comes Alive!

DID YOU KNOW?

Staten Island is "the greenest borough"—it has more than 170 parks!

1 LET'S GET STARTED

First, visit:
historicrichmondtown.org

New Places! New Words!

Look up the definition of these words before you go!

- apprentice • artisan
- artifact • skilled trade

2 ON THE WAY

Travel Talk

- How were children's lives different during the 1700s and 1800s?
- Without electric lights, which activities would be the most difficult to do?
- How did people share news with others before phones and the internet?

3 NOW YOU ARE HERE

What Does This Do?

Find an object from the past you don't recognize. Can you guess how it was used?

Snap a Pic!

Take a picture of a building you like. When was it built? Why do you like it?

4 ON THE WAY HOME

Thinking It Over!

- What surprised you about Richmond Town?
- How were people's lives in Richmond Town similar to and different from life today?
- Describe five objects from your life that you would want someone from the future to know about. Why did you choose those objects?

CAREER FLASH The following careers relate to experiencing Richmond Town. Do you know what each profession does?

- **Arborist** • **Historical interpreter**
- **Landscaper** • **Tinsmith**

Pick careers to research. What skills and education are needed to pursue these careers?

49

HUDSON RIVER PARK

Along the River, from Battery Park to W. 59th Street, Manhattan, (212) 627-2020   VISIT: hudsonriverpark.org

ADMISSION
Free*
*Additional activities' prices vary.

HOURS
6 AM–1 AM*
*Some areas, including playgrounds, close at dusk.

HOW TO GET HERE
Subway*: Ⓐ Ⓒ Ⓔ Ⓕ
Ⓜ Ⓝ Ⓠ Ⓡ Ⓢ
① ② ③ ⑦

Bus*: M8 M21 M23
M31 M42 M50 M57

*Check website for best transportation option based on targeted park location.

FOR SPECIAL NEEDS
Wheelchair accessible

SHELLEY REPORTS

Take a stroll, ride a scooter or bike, or catch a fish along this riverside park stretching from Battery Park to W. 59th Street. There are all types of land and water activities to explore.

- **KAYAKING** See NYC from a new view! During warm weather, launch from Pier 26 or 96 to kayak for free on the Hudson River. Pretty cool!

- **CHELSEA PIERS** This place is a sports lover's dream! With everything from a golf driving range to indoor ice skating to bowling, there are countless ways to play.

- **TRAPEZE SCHOOL** This high-flying adventure will fill you with a sense of wonder and adventure during the warm-weather months! (For ages 6+)

- **MINI GOLF** Located at Pier 25, it's the only 18-hole mini-golf course in Manhattan! Featuring waterfalls and a cave, it's a fun attraction for all!

MORE INFO: **ShelleysLearningAdventures.com**

SHELLEY'S ACTIVITIES
Water, Water Everywhere!

DID YOU KNOW?

The kayak was created by the Inuit native people long ago. Their kayaks were made from wooden or whalebone frames covered in sealskin.

③ NOW YOU ARE HERE
Water Craft
Take photos of the various boats you see. Describe their purpose.

Peek Inside!
At Clinton Cove, peek inside the windows of the giant bottle sculpture. What do you see inside?

① LET'S GET STARTED

First, visit: hudsonriverpark.org

New Places! New Words!
Look up the definition of these words before you go!

- bikeway
- ecology
- pier
- wildlife

② ON THE WAY
Travel Talk

- What is your favorite sport to play? Why do you like it?
- Why do you think it's important to take time to play and get exercise?
- How are rivers important to people and wildlife?

④ ON THE WAY HOME
Thinking It Over

- Animals enjoy the park too! What animals did you see there?
- If you could design a new area of the park for children, what would it include?
- Why is it important for our neighborhoods to have parks?

CAREER FLASH — The following careers relate to the Hudson River Park. Do you know what each profession does?

- Horticulturist
- Kayak instructor
- Landscape architect
- Parks and Recreation director
- Regional planner

What skills and education are needed to pursue these careers?

NEARBY → **MUSEUM OF JEWISH HERITAGE** 36 BATTERY PLACE *PAGE 72*
SKYSCRAPER MUSEUM 39 BATTERY PLACE *PAGE 116*

ADMISSION
NYC Residents:
Children: *(5–12)*: $17
Adults: $19
*Driver's license or NY
City ID required*

HOURS
DAILY including holidays,
10 AM–5 PM
*(Open until 6 PM Sat., Sun.,
and holidays, Apr.–Oct.)*

HOW TO GET HERE
Subway:
(A)(C)(E) N Q R
(S)(1)(2)(3) 7
Bus: M34 M42 M50

FOR SPECIAL NEEDS
lslearn.info/intrepid

SHELLEY REPORTS

Step aboard this historic aircraft
carrier! Imagine yourself at sea
standing on its huge flight deck. See
the awesome aircraft, including the
space shuttle *Enterprise*.

- **FLIGHT DECK** Get up close to a variety of planes, an
Avenger torpedo bomber, a Vietnam-era helicopter,
and other spectacular aircraft.

- **SPACE SHUTTLE PAVILION** Take a look at the
Enterprise, the magnificent space shuttle prototype,
and admire its gigantic size and majesty.

- **SUBMARINE GROWLER** Climb aboard a real
nuclear submarine, the USS *Growler*. Discover sailors'
tiny living quarters, a periscope, and a fascinating
control room!

- **THE EXPLOREUM** Jump in and take control as the
captain of a submarine or the pilot of a jet.

MORE INFO: **ShelleysLearningAdventures.com**

SHELLEY'S ACTIVITIES
Aboard a GIANT Aircraft Carrier!

DID YOU KNOW?

Space shuttles travel around Earth so quickly that astronauts can see a sunrise or sunset every 45 minutes!

① LET'S GET STARTED

First, visit: intrepidmuseum.org

New Places! New Words!

Look up the definition of these words before you go!

- aircraft carrier
- orbit
- periscope
- supersonic

② ON THE WAY
Travel Talk

- Why were submarines built to travel under the sea?
- What is life like for an astronaut in space?
- What is life like for a sailor living on an aircraft carrier?

③ NOW YOU ARE HERE
So Many Selfies!

Take a pic standing under the *Enterprise*, sitting in a helicopter, or exploring the sub. Share with your family!

Let's Jet!

Pretend you're a jet pilot. Estimate how long a flight would take to three different cities you select.

④ ON THE WAY HOME
Thinking It Over

- What would be the hardest part of living on a submarine?
- Would you rather pilot a space shuttle, military jet, or submarine?
- What can astronauts learn about Earth while in outer space?

CAREER FLASH The following careers relate to the Intrepid Sea, Air & Space Museum. Do you know what each profession does?

- **Aircraft restoration specialist**
- **Fighter aircraft mechanic** • **Jet pilot**
- **Submarine sonar technician**

What skills and education are needed to pursue these careers?

NEARBY → HUDSON RIVER PARK ENTER ON 46TH STREET *PAGE 50*
PREGONES THEATER/PUERTO RICAN TRAVELING THEATER 304 W. 47TH STREET *PAGE 104*

JAZZ STANDARD YOUTH ORCHESTRA (JSYO)

Jazz Standard, 116 E. 27th Street, Manhattan, (212) 576-2232   VISIT: discoverjazz.org

SHELLEY REPORTS

Come and swing with the Jazz Standard Youth Orchestra, where you'll hear some of the most talented young jazz musicians in the city!

ADMISSION
$5 suggested donation

PERFORMANCES
SUN. 2 PM–3 PM, Sep.-May only

HOW TO GET HERE
Subway: R W 6

Bus: X10 X10B X17 M101 M102 M103 BM1 BM2 BM3 BM4 M1 M2 M3 X63 X64 X68

FOR SPECIAL NEEDS
lslearn.info/jazzorch

- **YOUTH ORCHESTRA** Every Sunday, come hear talented children and top musicians perform famous numbers by artists such as Dizzy Gillespie and Miles Davis.

- **AUDITION!** Showtime! Every fall you can audition to play in the Jazz Band Youth Orchestra! To find out more, contact: info@keyedup.org.

- **BLUE SMOKE RESTAURANT** Baby back ribs, hot buttermilk biscuits, and banana pudding are some of the Southern classics you can taste at this restaurant!

SHELLEY'S ACTIVITIES
Bop and Swing to Real Jazz!

DID YOU KNOW?
Studies have shown that listening to jazz music can increase creativity and reduce stress!

③ NOW YOU ARE HERE
See the Different Styles
Compare and contrast the different playing styles of the musicians.

Get Moving
The band leader loves audience interaction! Get up and dance, or stand on stage to hear how the music sounds there!

① LET'S GET STARTED
First, visit: discoverjazz.org

New Places! New Words!
Look up the definition of these words before you go!

- bassline
- improvise
- jam session
- jazz music

② ON THE WAY
Travel Talk
- Do you like music that doesn't have words? Why?
- What types of instruments do you expect to find in a jazz orchestra?

④ ON THE WAY HOME
Thinking It Over
- What emotions do you think the JSYO children felt while performing on stage?
- How does music express feelings without using words?
- What different skills are needed to become an accomplished jazz musician?

CAREER FLASH

The following careers relate to the JSYO. Do you know what each profession does?

- Catering manager • House bandleader
- Jazz composer • Live sound engineer
- Pianist

Pick careers to research. What skills and education are needed to pursue these careers?

 NEARBY

NATIONAL MUSEUM OF MATHEMATICS 11 E. 26TH STREET *PAGE 80*
THE MUSEUM AT FASHION INSTITUTE OF TECHNOLOGY 7TH AVENUE AT 27TH STREET *PAGE 138*

LIBERTY SCIENCE CENTER
Liberty State Park, 222 Jersey City Boulevard,
Jersey City, New Jersey, (201) 200-1000
VISIT: lsc.org

GENERAL ADMISSION
Children *(under 2):* Free
Children *(2–12):* $18.75
Adults *(13+):* $22.75
Seniors *(62+):* $19.75

With Planetarium:
Children: $23.75
Adults: $28.75
Seniors: $25.75

HOURS
MON.–FRI. 9 AM–4 PM
SAT.– SUN. 9 AM–5:30 PM
Hours change seasonally, check website before you go!

HOW TO GET HERE
PATH Train/HBLR, car, and ferry directions: lsc.org/visit/directions

FOR SPECIAL NEEDS
lslearn.info/libscience

SHELLEY REPORTS

From the largest planetarium in the Western Hemisphere, to live animals, tornado-force wind simulators, and interactive STEM exhibits, this place never gets boring.

- **JENNIFER CHALSTY PLANETARIUM** Pretend you're an astronaut on a dazzling, colorful trip soaring past stars, planets, and distant galaxies!

- **SKYSCRAPER!** Walk across a narrow steel beam, face hurricane-force winds, and more as you explore the wonder of how skyscrapers are designed and built.

- **TOUCH TUNNEL** How would you escape a pitch-black tunnel? This exhibit is literally a hands-on experience— use your sense of touch to get out!

- **OUR HUDSON HOME** Get up close and personal with the fish, turtles, and shellfish that are all part of the Hudson River ecosystem.

MORE INFO: **ShelleysLearningAdventures.com**

SHELLEY'S ACTIVITIES
Science, Stars, and Skyscrapers!

DID YOU KNOW?

The moon doesn't have wind or rain—footprints left by astronauts will remain there forever.

③ NOW YOU ARE HERE

High Jinks!

In the Infinity Climber, get a photo acting silly as you climb 35 feet in the air!

So Many Species!

Count how many different animal species you can name as you explore the Science Center.

① LET'S GET STARTED

First, visit: lsc.org

New Places! New Words!

Look up the definition of these words before you go!

- cosmic
- ecosystem
- infinity
- pixel

④ ON THE WAY HOME

Thinking It Over

- Name three ways animals have evolved to protect themselves from predators.
- Would you live on Mars if given the chance? Why?
- What are some ways science can improve people's lives?

② ON THE WAY

Travel Talk

- Which of your senses would be hardest to live without? Why?
- Compare and contrast life on Earth with life on the moon.
- What animals do you think live in or around the Hudson River?

CAREER FLASH The following careers relate to Liberty Science Center. Do you know what each profession does?

- **Digital communications coordinator**
- **Herpetologist**
- **Infectious disease specialist**
- **Mammal keeper** • **STEM educator**

Pick careers to research. What skills and education are needed to pursue these careers?

NEARBY → **STATUE OF LIBERTY** LIBERTY ISLAND *PAGE 126*

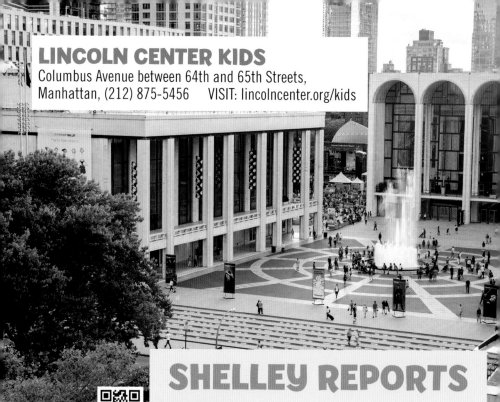

LINCOLN CENTER KIDS

Columbus Avenue between 64th and 65th Streets, Manhattan, (212) 875-5456   VISIT: lincolncenter.org/kids

ADMISSION

Ticket prices vary by performance. Check the website for performance dates, times, locations, and tickets.

HOW TO GET HERE

Subway: Ⓐ Ⓒ ❶

Bus: M5 M7 M10 M11 M66 M104

Find a children-friendly map of Lincoln Center at: lincolncenter.org/kids/faq

FOR SPECIAL NEEDS

lslearn.info/linckids

SHELLEY REPORTS

Lincoln Center is not just for grown-ups! Did you know they have the most sensational free and low-cost theater, music, and dance programs designed just for children?

- **PERFORMANCES!** Build a lifelong love of the arts by enjoying a wonderful variety of fantastic shows!

- **DAVID RUBENSTEIN ATRIUM** On the first Saturday of each month, catch free family-friendly performances in this beautiful, airy space.

- **REVSON FOUNTAIN** Be sure to check out the fountain's "water ballets"—towering sprays of water set to music!

- **AUTISM-FRIENDLY PERFORMANCES** Through the choice of sounds, lighting, and interactive elements, many shows at LC Kids are designed to be enjoyed by all children!

SHELLEY'S ACTIVITIES
A World of Performances!

DID YOU KNOW?

The NYC Ballet always keeps one stage light on—they say it's to keep the theater's ghosts happy!

① LET'S GET STARTED

First, visit: lincolncenter.org/kids

New Places! New Words!

Look up the definition of these words before you go!

- chamber music
- composer
- performing arts
- philharmonic

② ON THE WAY
Travel Talk

- In what ways do different types of music convey different emotions?
- Why are the performing arts important to people?
- How do dancers tell a story through their movements?

③ NOW YOU ARE HERE
Waterworks

Snap a selfie sitting on the edge of the famous Revson Fountain. It's so NYC!

Download It!

Download the free Tour Lincoln Center app to experience a fascinating audio tour as you explore!

④ ON THE WAY HOME
Thinking It Over

- How does a performing arts center benefit neighborhoods and communities?
- Compare and contrast seeing a live performance with watching or listening to one at home.

CAREER FLASH

The following careers relate to Lincoln Center. Do you know what each profession does?

- Assistant treasurer • Ballet dancer
- Community engagement program manager
- Front-end developer • Orchestra conductor

Pick careers to research. What skills and education are needed to pursue these careers?

NEARBY → CENTRAL PARK ENTER VIA 66TH STREET *PAGE 20*
SPYSCAPE 928 8TH AVENUE *PAGE 122*

LONG ISLAND CITY
Queens   VISIT: longislandcityqueens.com

SHELLEY REPORTS

With spectacular waterfront views, wonderful playgrounds and parks, great art museums, and lots of fun things to do, LIC is the perfect place to explore by foot or ferry!

ADMISSION
Free*
*Additional activities' prices vary.

HOW TO GET HERE
Subway: **E** **F** **G** **M** **N** **Q** **R** **7**

Bus: B62 Q39 Q66 Q67 Q69 Q100 QM20

Ferry: ferry.nyc/routes-and-schedules/

FOR SPECIAL NEEDS
Wheelchair accessible

- **GANTRY PLAZA STATE PARK** Take a walk along the East River and enjoy the views of Manhattan. Head north for several blocks and take a look at the amazing giant Pepsi Cola sign!

- **THE CLIFFS AT LIC** Get out all your energy at this indoor rock-climbing gym. (For pricing, visit: lic.thecliffsclimbing.com)

- **MoMA PS1** Featuring experimental, interactive art and changing exhibits, paired with child-friendly offerings including art workshops. (For pricing, visit: momaps1.org).

SHELLEY'S ACTIVITIES
LIC: On the Waterfront!

DID YOU KNOW?

Gantry cranes were used to lift railroad cars onto barges to transport products before trucks and tunnels were built.

① LET'S GET STARTED

First, visit:
longislandcityqueens.com

New Places! New Words!

Look up the definition of these words before you go!

- belay
- gantry crane
- plaza
- skyline

② ON THE WAY
Travel Talk

- Why might someone choose to take a ferry to LIC instead of a car or the subway?
- Why is it important for NYC residents to have easy access to parks and playgrounds?

③ NOW YOU ARE HERE
Beach Party!

Next to the ferry landing, hop in the sand at LIC's "beach," a giant sandbox area that's perfect for playing!

Cool Off

In warmer months, escape the heat while having a blast in Murray Playground's spray showers!

④ ON THE WAY HOME
Thinking It Over

- How do you think people traveled from Queens to Manhattan before there were bridges or subways?
- What would you do to make the Long Island City waterfront even more fun for children?

CAREER FLASH

The following careers relate to experiencing Long Island City. Do you know what each profession does?

- Ferry boat captain
- Neon sign builder
- Park ranger
- Urban planner

Pick careers to research. What skills and education are needed to pursue these careers?

LOUIS ARMSTRONG HOUSE MUSEUM

34-56 107th Street, Queens,
(718) 478-8274

VISIT: louisarmstronghouse.org

ADMISSION
Children *(under 5)*: Free
Students *(ID required)*: $7
Adults: $10
Seniors *(65+)*: $7

HOURS
TUES.–FRI.
10 AM–5 PM
SAT.–SUN.
12 PM–5 PM
Closed on Mon.
The museum is only shown through 40-minute house tours. Tours start every hour on the hour.

HOW TO GET HERE
Subway: **7**

Bus: Q66 Q48 Q22

FOR SPECIAL NEEDS
lslearn.info/armstrong

SHELLEY REPORTS

Visit the home of Louis Armstrong, America's most celebrated jazz musician, to learn all about his music and his love of his neighborhood.

- **TOUR THE HOUSE** Step into the house that Armstrong and his wife loved so much. With turquoise cabinets and a gold bathroom, their home will wow you!

- **ARMSTRONG'S ARTIFACTS** The collection of "Satchmo's Stuff" includes Louis's gold-plated trumpet and collages that Armstrong made in his free time.

- **PHOTOS AND SOUND RECORDINGS** Listen to Armstrong's trumpeting and see photos from his famous life. It's like time travel!

- **SUMMER CONCERTS** Swing to the sounds of big band jazz at summer concerts held in Armstrong's garden. Some concerts feature NYC's most talented high school jazz musicians!

MORE INFO: **ShelleysLearningAdventures.com**

SHELLEY'S ACTIVITIES
What a Wonderful Home!

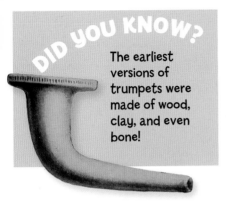

DID YOU KNOW?

The earliest versions of trumpets were made of wood, clay, and even bone!

1 LET'S GET STARTED

First, visit: louisarmstronghouse.org

New Places! New Words!

Look up the definition of these words before you go!

- collage
- jazz
- melody
- rhythm
- sheet music
- syncopation

2 ON THE WAY
Travel Talk

- Try improvising your own song!
- What are the differences between these types of instruments: brass, woodwind, percussion, and strings?

3 NOW YOU ARE HERE
Hum That Tune

Listen to one of Armstrong's songs being played, then take turns humming it back out loud.

What's Your Favorite?

Which room in the house is your favorite? Take a selfie in it!

4 ON THE WAY HOME
Thinking It Over

- Armstrong and his wife loved their neighborhood. What do you like about yours?
- When listening to Armstrong's music, how did it make you feel?
- One of Armstrong's most famous songs is "What a Wonderful World." What things in your life are wonderful?

CAREER FLASH

These careers relate to the Louis Armstrong House Museum. Do you know what each profession does?

- Composer
- Interior designer
- Landscaper
- Lyricist
- Record producer

Pick careers to research. What skills are needed to pursue these careers?

METROPOLITAN MUSEUM OF ART

1000 5th Avenue, Manhattan, (212) 535-7710   VISIT: metmuseum.org

ADMISSION
New York State residents: Pay what you wish.

Visitors from outside NY:
Children *(under 12)*: Free
Students: $12
Adults: $25
Seniors *(65+)*: $17

HOURS
SUN.–THUR.
10 AM–5:30 PM
FRI.–SAT. 10 AM–9 PM

HOW TO GET HERE
Subway: ④ ⑤ ⑥

Bus: M1 M2 M3 M4 M79 M86

FOR SPECIAL NEEDS
lslearn.info/met

SHELLEY REPORTS

From the great Temple of Dendur, to knights in shining armor, to paintings, sculptures, and artifacts—there are so many things to view, you'll want to return here again and again!

- **PAINTINGS** Swirling Van Gogh landscapes, *Washington Crossing the Delaware*, and Degas's dancers are just a few of the world-famous pieces on display.

- **EGYPTIAN ART** Visit an ancient Egyptian tomb and be amazed by mummies, Sphinx statues, and more!

- **ARMS AND ARMOR** View full sets of armor—for people and horses—a gold helmet sculpted like a lion's head, and gear such as sabers.

- **MUSICAL INSTRUMENTS** A brass and conch-shell trumpet, an instrument shaped like a peacock, and the oldest surviving piano are highlights of this exhibit!

MORE INFO: **ShelleysLearningAdventures.com**

SHELLEY'S ACTIVITIES
Masterpieces at the Met!

DID YOU KNOW?

Ancient Egyptians enjoyed playing board games. King Tut was buried with at least four boxes of games in his tomb!

① LET'S GET STARTED

First, visit: metmuseum.org

New Places! New Words!

Look up the definition of these words before you go!

- armor
- pictograph
- sarcophagus
- vessel

② ON THE WAY
Travel Talk

- How do cultures pass down stories about people's lives and beliefs through art?

- Why are visitors generally not allowed to touch the paintings and sculptures displayed at art museums?

③ NOW YOU ARE HERE
Tracking Time

Make a timeline featuring your favorite pieces! What periods of time were they from?

Observe This!

View a painting at the Met from a far distance, then look at it up close. What can you learn from both viewpoints?

④ ON THE WAY HOME
Thinking It Over

- How could people identify someone wearing armor even when their face was covered?

- Can you think of ways to make a musical instrument using objects from around your house?

CAREER FLASH The following careers relate to the Metropolitan Museum of Art. Do you know what each profession does?

- Art appraiser • Chief philanthropy officer
- Curator • E-commerce product specialist
- Objects conservation manager

Pick careers to research. What skills and education are needed to pursue these careers?

MOUNT VERNON HOTEL MUSEUM AND GARDEN

421 E. 61st Street, Manhattan,
(212) 838-6878   VISIT: mvhm.org

ADMISSION
Children *(under 13)*: Free
Children *(13–17)*: $8
Students *(ID required)*: $7
Adults: $8
Seniors *(62+)*: $7

HOURS
TUE.–SUN. 11 AM–4 PM

HOW TO GET HERE
Subway:
Ⓕ Ⓝ Ⓡ ④ ⑤ ⑥

Bus: M15 M31 M57

FOR SPECIAL NEEDS
lslearn.info/mtvernon

SHELLEY REPORTS

Believe it or not, over 150 years ago, this East Side hotel was once a vacation destination for people living in lower Manhattan. You'll find out why!

- **TAKE THE TOUR** As you explore the hotel's fascinating history, interact with its "touch collection"—reproductions of household objects from the 1800s!

- **GARDEN** Behind the house is a quaint garden. During warm months, test out the 18th- and 19th-century toys, like "hoop and stick"!

- **DRESS UP** Try on dresses, a cloak, boys' pants covered in buttons, and more! All clothing is inspired by what children wore in the 1800s. How fun!

- **SPECIAL EVENTS** With cool events like Teddy Bear Tea Party and an Ice Cream Social, there's lots of excitement to be had!

MORE INFO: **ShelleysLearningAdventures.com**

SHELLEY'S ACTIVITIES
Tour a Hotel from the 1800s!

DID YOU KNOW?

In the 1800s, not everyone had a fireplace. Most people used "bed-warmers" to keep warm at night.

① LET'S GET STARTED

First, visit: mvhm.org

New Places! New Words!

Look up the definition of these words before you go!

- bellows
- carriage house
- resort
- wick

② ON THE WAY

Travel Talk

- How did children have fun in the 1800s, before video games and TV?
- What household devices do you use every day that did not exist in the 1800s?

③ NOW YOU ARE HERE

Nature Wows!

In the garden, write a poem describing what a child would like about the hotel long ago.

Making Music

Check out the French barrel organ. Does it remind you of any modern music-making technology?

④ ON THE WAY HOME

Thinking It Over

- Can you name some "technologies" that existed in the 1800s?
- The neighborhood around the hotel was very different during the 1800s! How do you think it looked?

CAREER FLASH

The following careers relate to hotels. Do you know what each profession does?

- Concierge
- Director of revenue management
- Food and beverage manager • Innkeeper
- Maintenance engineer

Pick careers to research. What skills and education are needed to pursue these careers?

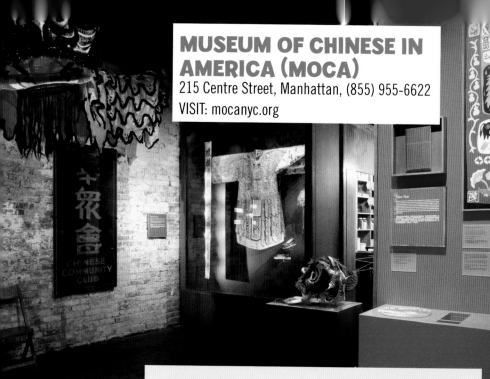

MUSEUM OF CHINESE IN AMERICA (MOCA)

215 Centre Street, Manhattan, (855) 955-6622

VISIT: mocanyc.org

ADMISSION
Children *(under 2)*: Free
Children *(2–12)*: $5
Students: $5
Adults: $10
Seniors *(65+)*: $5

HOURS
TUES.–SUN.
11 AM–6 PM
THUR. 11 AM–9 PM

HOW TO GET HERE
Subway: J N Q R
W Z 6

Bus: M9 M15 M103

FOR SPECIAL NEEDS
lslearn.info/moca

SHELLEY REPORTS

Explore the remarkable journey of the Chinese community in America. Artifacts and exhibits reveal powerful stories of their hardships and contributions to our nation.

- **LEARNING CENTER** Touch a century-old sewing machine and learn about the foods and spices in Chinese cooking to discover the unique history of Chinatown in this interactive exhibit. Wow!

- **"WITH A SINGLE STEP"** Discover Chinese Americans' unique personal stories that reveal the triumphs and challenges of immigrants building lives in America.

- **MOCACREATE** Experiment with fun hands-on crafts and express creativity through guided activities inspired by the museum's unique art collection.

MORE INFO: **ShelleysLearningAdventures.com**

SHELLEY'S ACTIVITIES
Chinese American History

DID YOU KNOW?

The dragon dance performed during Chinese festivals symbolizes good luck, wisdom, power, and prosperity.

③ NOW YOU ARE HERE
Photo Op!
Strike a pose wearing historical props at Our Chinatown Learning Center to create your very own old studio portrait.

Vlog It!
After watching the videos on display, make your own vlog about what you learned!

① LET'S GET STARTED

First, visit: mocanyc.org

New Places! New Words!
Look up the definition of these words before you go!

- hardships
- heritage
- journey
- prosperity

④ ON THE WAY HOME
Thinking It Over
- What five possessions would you take to settle in a new country?
- When people move to a new country, what challenges do they face?

② ON THE WAY
Travel Talk
- Why might people leave other countries to come and live in the United States?
- What does the word "home" mean to you?
- What is your family's heritage? Did any family members immigrate to the United States?

CAREER FLASH The following careers relate to the Museum of Chinese in America. Do you know what each profession does?

- Director of collections
- Grants coordinator
- Multimedia producer
- Technology coordinator

Pick careers to research. What skills and education are needed to pursue these careers?

NEARBY AFRICAN BURIAL GROUND NATIONAL MONUMENT 290 BROADWAY *PAGE 2*
TENEMENT MUSEUM 103 ORCHARD STREET *PAGE 132*

MUSEUM OF FOOD AND DRINK LAB

62 Bayard Street, Brooklyn, (718) 387-2845   VISIT: mofad.org

SHELLEY REPORTS

> In this quirky, wild, and fun museum, you can actually touch, taste, and smell the exhibits! You'll learn all about food and how it connects us to other cultures, communities, and each other.

ADMISSION
Children *(under 6)*: Free
Children *(6–17)*: $7
Adults: $14
Seniors *(60+)*: $10

HOURS
FRI.–SUN. 12 PM–6 PM

HOW TO GET HERE
Subway: G L
Bus: B43 B48 B62

FOR SPECIAL NEEDS
lslearn.info/
musfooddrink

- **CHANGING EXHIBITS** A "puffing gun" used to make cereal and a smelling and flavor exhibit to excite your senses are the types of displays featured at this very tasty museum!

- **TAKE A TASTE** Enjoy different food tastings every month to experience the tastes and smells of cultures around the world.

- **IN THE KITCHEN** Savor chef demos, hands-on workshops, and cooking classes made just for children!

- **COOKING AND FOOD ARTIFACTS** Learn all about the passion and interest people have had in food and cooking equipment from long ago to today.

MORE INFO: **ShelleysLearningAdventures.com**

SHELLEY'S ACTIVITIES
Food, Flavor, and History!

DID YOU KNOW?

Many popular Chinese dishes in the US—like egg rolls—didn't actually originate in China!

① LET'S GET STARTED

First, visit: mofad.org

New Places! New Words!
Look up the definition of these words before you go!

- culinary
- olfactory
- umami
- wok

② ON THE WAY
Travel Talk

- Why is some food at international restaurants different from the foods served in those countries?

- What role do research and product development scientists play at food companies?

③ NOW YOU ARE HERE
Take a Whiff!
At the scent machine, press the buttons to experience thousands of unique food and chemical aromas!

Taste Test!
The museum offers a different delicious food tasting every month, so you can taste the culinary world from your plate!

④ ON THE WAY HOME
Thinking It Over

- What is your favorite food? Why do you like it?

- How can you learn about different cultures through food?

- How do chefs show their personalities through the foods they cook?

CAREER FLASH The following careers relate to the Museum of Food and Drink Lab. Do you know what each profession does?

- Chef • Culinary historian
- Food scientist • Food writer
- Restaurant critic

Pick careers to research. What skills and education are needed to pursue these careers?

MUSEUM OF JEWISH HERITAGE

Edmond J. Safra Plaza, 36 Battery Place, Manhattan,
(646) 437-4202   VISIT: mjhnyc.org

SHELLEY REPORTS

> This museum is a memorial to the Holocaust. Artifacts, photos, videos, and powerful survivor testimony tell the story of the tragic history and renewal of the Jewish people.

ADMISSION
Children *(under 12)*: Free
Children *(14-18)*: $7
Students *(18+)*: $7
Adults: $12
Seniors *(65+)*: $10

HOURS
SUN.–TUES.
10 AM–6 PM
WED.–THUR.
10 AM–8 PM
FRI. 10 AM–5 PM

HOW TO GET HERE
Subway: R 1 4 5

Bus: M5 M9 M15 M20

FOR SPECIAL NEEDS
lslearn.info/
musjewheritage

- **LIFE A CENTURY AGO** Through artifacts, photos, videos, and more, discover the vibrant culture and history of Jewish people before WWII.

- **THE WAR AGAINST THE JEWS** Learn about the history of the Holocaust and how Jewish people were persecuted by the Nazis.

- **RENEWAL** See stories of Holocaust survivors, remember those who lost their lives, and explore how Jewish people rebuilt their communities after WWII.

- **GARDEN OF STONES** Trees grow from the top of giant boulders in this outdoor healing garden. It's a nice, quiet space for relaxing and reflecting.

MORE INFO: **ShelleysLearningAdventures.com**

SHELLEY'S ACTIVITIES
Remembering the Holocaust

DID YOU KNOW?

Even today, millions of people around the world are still persecuted for their religious beliefs.

1 LET'S GET STARTED

First, visit: mjhnyc.org

New Places! New Words!

Look up the definition of these words before you go!

- concentration camp
- holocaust • persecution
- tolerance

2 ON THE WAY
Travel Talk

- If you saw someone being bullied because of what they believe, how would you respond?

- What does it mean for all people to be treated equally?

3 NOW YOU ARE HERE
Get the Guide!

At the Welcome Desk, take a free children's museum guide. It'll show you how to use artifacts to discover your own family's heritage.

Video Narratives

Hear history firsthand by viewing the videos featuring Holocaust survivors.

4 ON THE WAY HOME
Thinking It Over

- Why is it important to remember the Holocaust?

- What steps can a person take to fight against persecution today?

CAREER FLASH

The following careers relate to the Museum of Jewish Heritage. Do you know what each profession does?

- **Director of leadership giving**
- **Museum curator • Photo restorer**

Pick careers to research. What skills and education are needed to pursue these careers?

NEARBY ▶ NATIONAL MUSEUM OF THE AMERICAN INDIAN ONE BOWLING GREEN *PAGE 82*
SKYSCRAPER MUSEUM 39 BATTERY PLACE *PAGE 116*

MUSEUM OF THE CITY OF NEW YORK

1220 5th Avenue, Manhattan,
(212) 534-1672
VISIT: mcny.org

ADMISSION

Suggested Admission:
Children *(under 19)*: Free
Students *(ID required)*: $12
Adults: $18
Seniors *(65+)*: $12

HOURS
DAILY 10 AM–6 PM

HOW TO GET HERE
Subway: ② ③ ⑥

Bus: M1 M2 M3
M4 M106

FOR SPECIAL NEEDS
lslearn.info/muscny

SHELLEY REPORTS

Take a fascinating walk through NYC history. Using art, video, photos, toys, and more, the past, present, and future of New York come together to celebrate its rich diversity!

- **NEW YORK AT ITS CORE** From a small Dutch village to today's "Capital of the World," explore the history of the most exciting city on Earth—NYC!

- *TIMESCAPES* History comes to life in this 28-minute film that takes you through New York City's colorful past and present!

- **STETTHEIMER DOLLHOUSE** This is a world-famous dollhouse! Built in the early 1900s and featuring miniature paintings from famous artists, it's so adorable.

- *STARLIGHT* Look up! This sculpture of more than 5,000 hanging lights in the museum's rotunda is extraordinary!

MORE INFO: **ShelleysLearningAdventures.com**

SHELLEY'S ACTIVITIES
Big Apple History!

DID YOU KNOW?

In 1863, Sarah J. Smith Thompson Garnet became the first African American female principal in the New York City public school system!

1 LET'S GET STARTED

First, visit: mcny.org

New Places! New Words!

Look up the definition of these words before you go!

- capital
- metropolis
- rotunda
- settlement

2 ON THE WAY
Travel Talk

- What makes NYC a "global city" today?
- Why do people call NYC "The City That Never Sleeps"?
- In the 1800s, how was NYC different from today?

3 NOW YOU ARE HERE
Starlight Selfie

The *Starlight* display is dazzling. Snap a picture with it!

Twins?

Search photographs and paintings—can you find someone that looks like you?

4 ON THE WAY HOME
Thinking It Over

- If you could live in NYC during a different time period, what period would you choose?
- Where would you take tourists or friends to show them your favorite NYC sights?
- Compare and contrast the best possible types of transportation to travel around New York City.

CAREER FLASH

The following careers relate to the Museum of the City of New York. Do you know what each profession does?

- **Graphic designer** • **Land surveyor**
- **Manager of events and beverages**
- **Real estate developer** • **Urban planner**

Pick careers to research. What skills and education are needed to pursue these careers?

NEARBY ➤ **CENTRAL PARK** ENTER AT 104TH STREET *PAGE 20*
EL MUSEO DEL BARRIO 1230 5TH AVENUE *PAGE 32*

MUSEUM OF THE MOVING IMAGE

36-01 35th Avenue, Queens, (718) 777-6888

VISIT: movingimage.us

ADMISSION*
Children *(under 3)*: Free
Children *(3–17)*: $9
Students *(18+)*: $11
Adults: $15
Seniors *(65+)*: $11
* Free on Fri. 4 PM–8 PM

HOURS
WED.–THUR.
10:30 AM–5 PM
FRI. 10:30 AM–8 PM
SAT.–SUN.
10:30 AM–6 PM

HOW TO GET HERE
Subway: M N R W

Bus: Q66 Q101

FOR SPECIAL NEEDS
lslearn.info/momi

SHELLEY REPORTS

Lights! Camera! Action! Step behind the camera lens to learn all about the fascinating world of filmmaking, TV production, digital media, and other kinds of entertainment.

- **BEHIND THE SCREEN** Get hands-on while discovering the magic of movies. Explore 1,400 fascinating film artifacts, like Chewbacca's mask, play video games, and record your voice like a real actor!

- **JIM HENSON EXHIBITION** Learn all about the puppets, character sketches, and costumes created by the famous Muppets creator Jim Henson. See Kermit, Miss Piggy, and more of your puppet friends.

- **DROP-IN MOVING IMAGE STUDIO** On most weekend days, join museum educators as they teach computer animation techniques, help you create optical toys, and do other fun film- and game-based projects!

MORE INFO: **ShelleysLearningAdventures.com**

SHELLEY'S ACTIVITIES
Movie and Video Game Fun!

DID YOU KNOW?

The movie industry in India, called "Bollywood," is the largest in the world. It makes over 800 movies a year! That is twice as many as Hollywood produces!

1 LET'S GET STARTED

First, visit: movingimage.us

New Places! New Words!

Look up the definition of these words before you go!

- animation
- film projector
- flipbook
- sound effect

2 ON THE WAY
Travel Talk

- If you made a movie about your life, what would you call it?
- Do you like movies or video games more? Why?
- How do computers and other technologies help filmmakers make movies?

3 NOW YOU ARE HERE
Pick a Puppet

In the Jim Henson Exhibition, take a selfie with your favorite Muppet or other puppet.

Direct It

At the Behind the Screen exhibit, add sound effects and music to movie scenes.

4 ON THE WAY HOME
Thinking It Over

- What skills are needed to create a film or video?
- Why is video game design a good career for artists, writers, and people who love math?
- How is telling a story through a movie different from telling a story through a book?

CAREER FLASH The following careers relate to the film and gaming industries. Do you know what each profession does?

- Animator
- Puppeteer
- Script supervisor
- Stop motion animator
- Video game developer

Pick careers to research. What skills and education are needed to pursue these careers?

NATIONAL GEOGRAPHIC ENCOUNTER: OCEAN ODYSSEY

226 W. 44th Street, Manhattan, (646) 308-1337

VISIT: natgeoencounter.com

ADMISSION

Children *(under 13)*: $32.50

Adults *(13+)*: $39.50

Seniors *(65+)*: $36.50

These costs are for reserved times. Flexible-entrance tickets have additional costs. See website for info.

HOURS

SUN.–THUR.
10 AM–9 PM

FRI.–SAT.
10 AM–10 PM

HOW TO GET HERE

Subway: A B C D E F M N Q R S 1 2 3 7

Bus: M7 M20 M104

FOR SPECIAL NEEDS

lslearn.info/natgeo

SHELLEY REPORTS

Dive into a thrilling digital underwater adventure where you will never get wet. You'll feel like you're really swimming with dolphins—and even big sharks!

- **FISH ON THE FLOOR!** Pretend you're a real shark swimming through a dazzling undersea world—chase fish across the floor and watch them scurry away.

- **KELP MAZE** Explore the ocean depths, weaving through a dense, magical forest of kelp. Be sure to say hello to the sea lion too. Pretty cool!

- **SQUID FIGHT!** Get a front-row view of a fierce battle between two Humboldt squid. Nicknamed "red devils," these huge squid weigh up to 110 pounds!

- **3-D GLASSES** Experience the immersive thrill of schools of fish, sea lions, and a whale charging toward you. It's wild in 3-D!

MORE INFO: **ShelleysLearningAdventures.com**

SHELLEY'S ACTIVITIES
Undersea Adventures!

DID YOU KNOW?

A giant squid's eyeball is 10.5 inches across. That's about the size of a Frisbee!

1 LET'S GET STARTED

First, visit: natgeoencounter.com

New Places! New Words!

Look up the definition of these words before you go!

- immersive
- kelp
- mammal
- odyssey

2 ON THE WAY
Travel Talk

- What effect does overfishing have on an ocean's food chain?
- Are oceans important to people in urban communities?
- How is the ocean different from lakes and rivers?

3 NOW YOU ARE HERE
Sea Music

Listen carefully as you explore. What different sounds do sea creatures make?

A-maze-ing Snaps!

Snap some pics of yourself in the kelp maze and chasing fish. Create a digital photo collage of your experience!

4 ON THE WAY HOME
Thinking It Over

- How do sea creatures protect themselves from predators?
- What skills do you need to become a marine biologist?
- Why is it important to protect the oceans and not pollute them?

CAREER FLASH The following careers relate to the Ocean Odyssey. Do you know what each profession does?

- Aquatic veterinarian
- Coastal preservation manager
- Oceanographer • Scuba instructor

Pick careers to research. What skills and education are needed to pursue these careers?

NEARBY GULLIVER'S GATE 216 W. 44TH STREET *PAGE 44*
THE NEW VICTORY THEATER 209 W. 42ND STREET *PAGE 140*

79

NATIONAL MUSEUM OF MATHEMATICS

11 E. 26th Street, Manhattan, (212) 542-0566   VISIT: momath.com

ADMISSION*

Children *(0–2)*: Free
Children *(3–12)*: $12
Students *(ID required)*: $12
Adults: $18
Seniors *(60+)*: $12

*Tickets purchased online
cost $1 less.*

HOURS

DAILY* 10 AM–5 PM

*Closes at 2:30 PM the
first Wed. of every month.*

HOW TO GET HERE

Subway:

Bus: M1 M2 M3 M23

FOR SPECIAL NEEDS

Wheelchair accessible

SHELLEY REPORTS

MoMath is the coolest thing to happen to math! With guides who explain the 40 interactive exhibits and touch screens everywhere, this place is a giant math amusement park!

- **HOOP CURVES** Hey there, nice shot! Come play with BallBot. It's a cool robot basketball machine that helps people shoot free throws—using math!

- **HARMONY OF SPHERES** Create cool sounds with this interactive musical sculpture.

- **SQUARE-WHEELED TRICYCLE** Sounds impossible, right? But, using rules of math and a special bumpy path, these trikes are real—and really fun!

- **ROBOT SWARM** Watch out for bots! In this fun exhibit, small, colorful robots "talk" to each other, then chase and zoom away from visitors.

MORE INFO: **ShelleysLearningAdventures.com**

SHELLEY'S ACTIVITIES
Having Fun with Math!

DID YOU KNOW?

A recent survey has found that seven is the world's favorite number.

① LET'S GET STARTED

First, visit: momath.org

New Places! New Words!

Look up the definition of these words before you go!

- algorithm
- data
- octagon
- perimeter

② ON THE WAY

Travel Talk

- Can you think of all the different ways we use math when we are making cookies?

- In what ways might people use math while grocery shopping?

- If you spend 15 minutes at each of the museum's 12 exhibits, how long will it take to go through the museum?

③ NOW YOU ARE HERE

Time for a Selfie!

Snap a pic in front of your Polypaint masterpiece to share with friends!

A Tree ... Made of Me?

At the Human Tree exhibit, discover how many branches you can create on your tree.

④ ON THE WAY HOME

Thinking It Over

- Imagine a square-wheeled trike on a flat road. Would it work? Why?

- Think of some sports besides basketball. How could math skillls help in those sports?

- If you could design a fun math-related museum exhibit, what would you create?

CAREER FLASH

These professionals all need math skills. Do you know how math is used in their jobs?

- **Architect** • **Astronaut**
- **Chef** • **Computer programmer**
- **Game designer**

Pick jobs to research. What math skills and education are needed to pursue these careers?

NEARBY → JAZZ STANDARD YOUTH ORCHESTRA 116 E. 27TH STREET *PAGE 54*
THE MUSEUM AT FASHION INSTITUTE OF TECHNOLOGY 7TH AVENUE & 27TH STREET *PAGE 138*

NATIONAL MUSEUM OF THE AMERICAN INDIAN

Alexander Hamilton US Custom House, One Bowling Green, Manhattan, (212) 514-3700

VISIT: nmai.si.edu/visit/newyork

ADMISSION
Free

HOURS
MON–WED., FRI.–SUN.
10 AM–5 PM
THUR. 10 AM–8 PM

HOW TO GET HERE
Subway: J R Z W
1 2 3 4 5

Bus: M5 M15 M20

FOR SPECIAL NEEDS
lslearn.info/
natmusamin

SHELLEY REPORTS

This collection of artifacts brings to life the culture and remarkable contributions of hundreds of tribes of native peoples of the Americas.

- **INFINITY OF NATIONS** Admire feathered headdresses, a beaded jacket, and more than 700 historical objects created by native peoples of the Americas.

- **imagiNATIONS ACTIVITY CENTER** From early versions of sunglasses and suspension bridges, to chocolate and sports like lacrosse—discover how native peoples of the Americas changed the way we live.

- **SEASONAL EVENTS** The museum hosts fun, child-friendly events throughout the year. Highlights include a Winter Blast, a children's festival in the spring, and a Summer Dance! event.

SHELLEY'S ACTIVITIES
Native People's Art & Inventions!

DID YOU KNOW?

During World War II, Navajo "code talkers" created a top-secret, unbreakable code for the US based on the Navajo language.

① LET'S GET STARTED

First, visit:
nmai.si.edu/visit/newyork

New Places! New Words!

Look up the definition of these words before you go!

- indigenous
- maize
- nomadic
- treaty

② ON THE WAY
Travel Talk

- What different continents or parts of the world make up the "Americas"?
- How can we learn about cultures throughout history without written records?

③ NOW YOU ARE HERE
Mayan Math!

Use the touch screen in the imagiNATIONS area to play fun games based on Mayan math principles!

Grab a Guide

At the museum entrance, pick up an Infinity of Nations guide to help you find cool objects in the exhibit!

④ ON THE WAY HOME
Thinking It Over

- How do native peoples of the Americas celebrate nature and the environment?
- What contributions to technology have native peoples of the Americas made throughout our history?

CAREER FLASH

The following careers relate to the National Museum of the American Indian. Do you know what each profession does?

- Cultural interpreter
- Education product developer
- Museum cultural specialist • Tribal liaison
- Tribal schoolteacher • Web developer

What skills and education are needed to pursue these careers?

NEARBY ➤ MUSEUM OF JEWISH HERITAGE 36 BATTERY PLACE *PAGE 72*
SKYSCRAPER MUSEUM 39 BATTERY PLACE *PAGE 116*

NEW YORK AQUARIUM
Surf Avenue & W. 8th Street, Brooklyn, NY 11224
(718) 220-5100   Visit: nyaquarium.com/visitor-info

ADMISSION
Children *(under 2)*: Free
Children *(2–12)*: $11.95
Adults: $14.95
Seniors *(60+)*: $12.95

HOURS
Hours vary by month
and season. Visit:
nyaquarium.com/hours

HOW TO GET HERE
Subway:

Bus: B36 B68

FOR SPECIAL NEEDS
lslearn.info/nyaqua

SHELLEY REPORTS

Wow! Get up close and personal with real sharks, rays, and sea turtles, and watch them as they swim right over your head!

- **OCEAN WONDERS: SHARKS!** There are 18 types of sharks, rays, and sea turtles, and over 115 other colorful marine life species to explore in this eye-popping and interactive exhibit!

- **CONSERVATION HALL** From fish and eels to coral reefs, you'll learn about an amazing variety of wildlife that inhabits our oceans!

- **SEA CLIFFS** Check out the adorable penguins, sea otters, and seals, and learn why many ocean species spend time on rocks and cliffs!

- **AQUA-THEATER** Watch sea lions being fed as they interact with their trainers and learn behaviors that help aid in their care.

MORE INFO: **ShelleysLearningAdventures.com**

SHELLEY'S ACTIVITIES
Discover Life Underwater!

DID YOU KNOW?

Not all sharks are vicious man-eaters. Only 10 out of the 400 shark species are dangerous to humans!

① LET'S GET STARTED

First visit: nyaquarium.com

New Places! New Words!

Look up the definition of these words before you go!

- colonies
- coral reef
- gills
- species
- sustainable

② ON THE WAY
Travel Talk

- Why do some species of fish become extinct?
- In what ways are the oceans important to people who live in coastal communities like New York City?

③ NOW YOU ARE HERE
Sea Guide!

Create a guide with photos and notes about the different aquatic animals you have seen!

No Plastic!

Play the interactive "Stomp the Trash" game in the shark exhibit while learning about the harmful effects of pollution.

④ ON THE WAY HOME
Thinking It Over

- How do aquariums keep each habitat safe and comfortable for aquatic animals?
- What are some ways to reduce waste and ensure that less plastic pollutes our oceans?
- What is the difference between a marine mammal and a fish?

CAREER FLASH

The following careers help support the New York Aquarium. Do you know what each profession does?

- Aquarist • Marine biologist
- Oceanographer • Sea trainer

What skills and education do you need to pursue these careers?

NEW YORK BOTANICAL GARDEN

2900 Southern Boulevard, Bronx,
(718) 817-8700   VISIT: nybg.org

ADMISSION

All-garden pass*:
Children *(under 2)*: Free
Children *(2–12)*:$12/$10
Students: $25/$20
Adults: $28/$23
Seniors *(65+)*: $25/$20
*Costs are for weekends/
weekdays.*

HOURS

TUES.–SUN.
10 AM–6 PM*
Winter closure: 5 PM

HOW TO GET HERE

Subway: **B** **D** **2** **4**

Train: Metro-North
Harlem local line

Bus: Bx19 Bx12 Bx22,
Bx9 Bx17 Bx26 Bx41
Bx34

FOR SPECIAL NEEDS

lslearn.info/nybotanical

SHELLEY REPORTS

Enjoy nature in the Bronx surrounded by beautiful gardens, plants, flowers, and trees. It's all so peaceful and quiet!

- **CHILDREN'S ADVENTURE GARDEN** Dash around boulders and through shrub mazes, explore the biodiversity of pond life, and more as you discover nature's wonders!

- **EDIBLE ACADEMY** Dig in the dirt and learn all about growing fruits and vegetables through hands-on gardening activities—and even cooking demonstrations!

- **THAIN FAMILY FOREST** Hike hunting trails used by native peoples of the Americas, admire a waterfall, and experience the majesty of gorgeous old-growth woods.

- **CONSERVATORY** In this magnificent glass structure, discover plants that grow in tropical rainforests and cactus-filled deserts.

SHELLEY'S ACTIVITIES
Green, Green in the Bronx!

DID YOU KNOW?

The Thain Family Forest is the largest piece of original forest remaining in NYC.

BRONX

$$

③ NOW YOU ARE HERE

Tram Time
Hop on the tram for a narrated tour of the garden's magnificent grounds!

Nature Scientist!
As you explore the gardens, take field notes and pictures along the way!

① LET'S GET STARTED
First, visit: nybg.org

New Places! New Words!
Look up the definition of these words before you go!

- biodiversity
- botanical
- conservatory
- energy conservation

② ON THE WAY
Travel Talk
- What do plants need to grow?
- Would you prefer to grow a flower garden or a vegetable garden? Why?
- How do we know the Earth's climate is changing?

④ ON THE WAY HOME
Thinking It Over
- Why is it important for humans to reduce their impact on the environment?
- What was the most unusual plant you saw while exploring the garden?

CAREER FLASH
The following careers relate to the New York Botanical Garden. Do you know what each profession does?

- Chief naturalist • Ethnobotanist
- Financial reporting manager
- Medicinal plant scientist
- Systems librarian

Pick careers to research. What skills and education are needed to pursue these careers?

NEARBY ➤ BRONX ZOO 2300 SOUTHERN BOULEVARD *PAGE 10*
BRONX ZOO TREETOP ADVENTURE BRONX RIVER PKWY AT BOSTON ROAD *PAGE 12*

87

NYC FERRY
E. 35th Street at FDR Drive, Manhattan,
(Various stops throughout NYC)   VISIT: ferry.nyc

ADMISSION
Adults *(one-way)*: $2.75
Bikes *(one-way)*: $1.00

HOURS
Check website for specific route times and to see ferry destinations. Most routes begin around 6 AM, conclude around 10 PM, and run a few times per hour.

HOW TO GET HERE
34th Street Landing*

Subway: **6**

Bus: M15 M34
Many more ferry landings are located throughout NYC!

FOR SPECIAL NEEDS
Wheelchair accessible

SHELLEY REPORTS

With names like Lunchbox and Friendship Express, these ferries must be special. So hop on and off and explore NYC's waterfront communities as you enjoy the spectacular views!

- **34TH STREET LANDING** From this Manhattan launching spot, hop on a ferry along the East River for a quick ride to many cool neighborhoods.

- **PLACES TO VISIT!** From the 34th Street landing, countless adventures await! The artsy DUMBO neighborhood, Gantry Plaza State Park, and Astoria's Socrates Sculpture Park are just a few amazing places close to ferry stops.

- **THE RIDE** With both outdoor and indoor seating, plus a shop to buy things like coloring books and snacks, this is one of the most comfortable and thrilling ways to travel around the city!

MORE INFO: **ShelleysLearningAdventures.com**

SHELLEY'S ACTIVITIES
Discover NYC by Ferry!

DID YOU KNOW?

NYC schoolchildren gave NYC Ferry boats their fun names, including *Unity* and *Seas the Day*!

Unity
Seas the Day

① LET'S GET STARTED

First, visit: ferry.nyc

New Places! New Words!

Look up the definition of these words before you go!

- ferry landing
- fuel efficiency
- nautical
- on board

② ON THE WAY
Travel Talk

- How do ferries help the businesses and people in NYC's waterfront communities?
- NYC Ferry boats are made to be fuel-efficient. Why is that important to consider?

③ NOW YOU ARE HERE
Wind-Blown Fun!

Stand outside on the upper deck and feel the wind blow through your hair. Snap a selfie!

You're the Expert

Take a tour of the ferry, then create a video review of the ferry, its features, and the ride itself.

④ ON THE WAY HOME
Thinking It Over

- Why is it important for NYC Ferry boats to have small wakes?
- In NYC, what might happen if everyone tried to drive cars instead of taking subways, buses, and ferries?
- If you designed a ferry, what features would you include?

CAREER FLASH

The following careers relate to NYC Ferry. Do you know what each profession does?

- Deckhand • Marine mechanic
- Naval architect • Ship captain

Pick careers to research. What skills and education are needed to pursue these careers?

NEARBY ➤ **LONG ISLAND CITY** TAKE 34TH STREET FERRY ONE STOP TO LONG ISLAND CITY *PAGE 60*
UNITED NATIONS 405 E. 42ND STREET *PAGE 144*

NEW YORK CITY FIRE MUSEUM

278 Spring Street, Manhattan,
(212) 691-1303

VISIT: nycfiremuseum.org

ADMISSION
Children *(under 2)*: Free
Children *(2–12)*: $5
Students: $5
Adults: $8
Seniors *(65+)*: $5

HOURS
DAILY 10 AM–5 PM

HOW TO GET HERE
Subway: C E 1

Bus: M10 M21

FOR SPECIAL NEEDS
lslearn.info/nycfire

SHELLEY REPORTS

Here's a real firehouse filled with historic firefighting trucks, equipment, uniforms, and more. Be a firefighter for a day and learn to be one of New York's bravest.

- **FIREFIGHTING ON PARADE** Check out the lanterns, hats, helmets, and even a horse carriage used by NYC firefighters in city parades starting in the 1800s.

- **FIRE APPARATUS** Get ready! See horse-drawn cars and steam engine vehicles, and experience the history of transportation for NYC firefighters.

- **TOOLS AND UNIFORMS** Learn how much firefighters' uniforms and tools have improved in the past 100 years. See helmets, axes, and other gear up close!

- **9/11 MEMORIAL** Pay tribute to the 343 firefighters who gave their lives to protect others on September 11, 2001. It's a powerful reminder of true heroes.

SHELLEY'S ACTIVITIES
Firefighting Up Close!

DID YOU KNOW?

Originally, Dalmatians were trained to run in front of fire-carriages to help clear the way during emergencies!

3 NOW YOU ARE HERE
Try It On!
Put on the firefighter's helmet and coat. How would it feel to wear the equipment during a fire?

Cool Tools!
In the tools area, pick a tool that you don't recognize and learn about how it's used.

1 LET'S GET STARTED
First, visit: nycfiremuseum.org

New Places! New Words!
Look up the definition of these words before you go!

- apparatus - carriage
- engine - hazard

4 ON THE WAY HOME
Thinking It Over
- How have firefighting methods changed over time?
- Why are people told to "stop, drop, and roll" if their clothes catch on fire?

2 ON THE WAY
Travel Talk
- What skills do firefighters need to have?
- Why do firefighters need to be healthy and fit?
- Do you want to be a firefighter one day? Why or why not?

CAREER FLASH

The following careers relate to the New York City Fire Museum. Do you know what each profession does?

- **Arson dog trainer** • **Fire chief**
- **Fire inspector** • **Forensic scientist**
- **Paramedic**

Pick careers to research. What skills and education are needed to pursue these careers?

NEARBY **CHILDREN'S MUSEUM OF THE ARTS** 103 CHARLTON STREET *PAGE 24*
HUDSON RIVER PARK ENTER ON CANAL STREET *PAGE 50*

NEW YORK HALL OF SCIENCE
47-01 111th Street, Queens, (718) 699-0005   VISIT: nysci.org

ADMISSION
Children *(under 2)*: Free
Children *(2–17)*: $13
Adults: $16
Students: $13
Seniors *(62+)*: $13
Additional admission required for 3-D theater, mini golf, and science playground.

HOURS
MON.–FRI.
9:30 AM–5 PM,
SAT.–SUN. 10 AM–6 PM

HOW TO GET HERE
Subway: **7**

Bus: Q23 Q48 Q58

FOR SPECIAL NEEDS
lslearn.info/
nyhallscience

SHELLEY REPORTS

This place never gets boring! Science is fun with more than 450 interactive exhibits, tons of hands-on learning activities, and "red-aproned" museum guides who are available to help.

- **CONNECTED WORLDS** Discover how your actions affect the Earth through stunning animated displays! Wave your hands to "plant" seeds or "move" a flowing waterfall, and interact with plants, animals, and more.

- **DESIGN LAB** Tinkerers and future engineers, check this out! Build structures and inventions using simple materials like pipe cleaners, circuits, and dowels. Through hands-on activities, learn how science and creativity can shape innovation!

- **THE SPORTS CHALLENGE** Race a drag car, try out rock climbing, catch a "wave," and pitch a ball! Through play and experimentation, explore the role of science and physics in sports.

MORE INFO: **ShelleysLearningAdventures.com**

SHELLEY'S ACTIVITIES
Having Fun with Science!

DID YOU KNOW?

The weight of an average cumulus cloud is about the same as 100 elephants!

1 LET'S GET STARTED

First, visit: nysci.org

New Places! New Words!

Look up the definition of these words before you go!

- friction
- biodiversity
- inertia
- momentum

2 ON THE WAY

Travel Talk

- How do you use water? Why is water also important to plants and animals?
- What is something you've built by yourself that made you proud?
- Name some ways you use math and science skills outside of school.

3 NOW YOU ARE HERE

Invent It!

In the Design Lab, create an invention with the available materials. What does it do?

Take Action!

At the Sports Challenge, get a photo "hanging 10" on the surfboard like a real surfer!

4 ON THE WAY HOME

Thinking It Over

- If you could create a cool invention, what would it do?
- Can you think of scientific developments that have improved a sport?
- Identify three things you can do to protect the environment.

 CAREER FLASH The following careers relate to the New York Hall of Science. Do you know what each profession does?

- **Aquatic biologist** • **Baseball hitting coach**
- **Industrial designer**
- **Sport biomechanist**

Pick careers to research. What skills and education are needed to pursue these careers?

NEARBY ➤ LOUIS ARMSTRONG HOUSE MUSEUM 34-56 107TH STREET *PAGE 62*
QUEENS MUSEUM FLUSHING MEADOWS CORONA PARK *PAGE 108*

NEW-YORK HISTORICAL SOCIETY/ DIMENNA CHILDREN'S HISTORY MUSEUM
170 Central Park West, Manhattan, (212) 873-3400   VISIT: nyhistory.org

ADMISSION
Children *(under 5)*: Free
Children *(5–13)*: $6
Students *(14+)*: $13
Adults: $21
Seniors *(65+)*: $16

HOURS
TUES.–THUR.
10 AM–6 PM
FRI. 10 AM–8 PM
SAT. 10 AM–6 PM
SUN. 11 AM–5 PM

HOW TO GET HERE
Subway: B C 1

Bus: M9 M10 M79
X1 X10 X28

FOR SPECIAL NEEDS
lslearn.info/nyhistsoc

SHELLEY REPORTS

Discover the history of America and New York through the remarkable stories of children from long ago. Artifacts and interactive exhibits make the past truly come to life!

- **CHILDREN'S MUSEUM** Through interactive displays, become a "history detective" to see how old objects give clues about the past.

- *NEW YORK STORY* This film uses sound, lighting, and visuals to take you on an enchanting tour through NYC's colorful history.

- **OBJECTS TELL STORIES** See how objects, such as George Washington's wartime cot and a copper globe from 1542, can share rich details about life long ago.

MORE INFO: **ShelleysLearningAdventures.com**

SHELLEY'S ACTIVITIES
Explore NYC's Rich History!

DID YOU KNOW?

In the 1800s, children often sold newspapers on NYC streets. They only made about 26 cents per day!

① LET'S GET STARTED

First, visit: nyhistory.org

New Places! New Words!

Look up the definition of these words before you go!

- artifact
- cot
- reenactment
- revolution

② ON THE WAY
Travel Talk

- Why is it important to limit how many hours children under 18 can work?
- Which of your daily activities would be similar to a child living hundreds of years ago?
- Why is it important to learn about people from long ago?

③ NOW YOU ARE HERE
Neat Tweet

Pretend you are a person from long ago and send a tweet to your friends about your life!

How Presidential!

In the children's museum, take a pic as George Washington at the inauguration photo op!

④ ON THE WAY HOME
Thinking It Over

- How is life for children today similar to and different from life in the 1700s and 1800s?
- In what ways do household objects teach us about living in NYC in the past?
- How has technology changed the way people work and play?

CAREER FLASH The following careers relate to the New-York Historical Society. Do you know what each profession does?

- AV operations specialist • Chief historian
- Educational research assistant
- Historical interpreter
- Manager of digital learning programs

What skills and education are needed to pursue these careers?

NEARBY ▶ AMERICAN MUSEUM OF NATURAL HISTORY 79TH STREET & CENTRAL PARK *PAGE 4*
CENTRAL PARK ENTER ON 77TH STREET *PAGE 22*

NY PUBLIC LIBRARY & LIBRARY WAY

Library Way: Between Park and Fifth Avenues on 41st Street

New York Public Library: Fifth Avenue & 42nd Street, Manhattan,

(917) 275-6975   VISIT: nypl.org

ADMISSION
Free

LIBRARY HOURS*
MON., THUR.–SAT.
10 AM–6 PM
TUES.–WED.
10 AM–8 PM
SUN. 1 PM–5 PM
Children's Center hours differ slightly. Check website for details.

HOW TO GET HERE
Subway: Ⓐ Ⓑ Ⓒ Ⓓ
Ⓔ Ⓕ Ⓜ Ⓝ Ⓠ Ⓡ
Ⓢ Ⓦ ④ ⑤ ⑥ ⑦

Bus: M1 M2 M3 M4
M5 M55 Q32 X1 X7
X9 X27 X28 X37
X38 X68

FOR SPECIAL NEEDS
lslearn.info/nypublib

SHELLEY REPORTS

Just stroll down 41st Street and follow the inspirational quotes embedded in the sidewalk and you'll be led right to the steps of this majestic library.

- **LIBRARY WAY** On your way, read the inspiring literary quotes etched in 96 bronze plaques along 41st Street.

- **PATIENCE & FORTITUDE** Two magnificent marble lion statues sit in front of the library. They are absolutely iconic. Don't miss getting a picture in front of one!

- **CHILDREN'S CENTER** See the real Winnie-the-Pooh, and lots of books for children of all ages to read!

- **AMAZING BUILDING** Incredible research rooms and a ceiling mural of pink clouds are some of the beautiful details in this beaux arts building!

MORE INFO: **ShelleysLearningAdventures.com**

SHELLEY'S ACTIVITIES
Books, Books, and Lions!

DID YOU KNOW?

Former New York City mayor Fiorello La Guardia named the library's lions "Patience" and "Fortitude" to inspire people in difficult times.

① LET'S GET STARTED

First, visit: nypl.org

New Places! New Words!

Look up the definition of these words before you go!

- beaux arts
- fortitude
- literacy
- patience

② ON THE WAY

Travel Talk

- The writer Ralph Waldo Emerson said, "Patience and fortitude conquer all things." What do you think he meant?
- Which book characters would you like to meet in real life? Why?

③ NOW YOU ARE HERE

So Quotable

Along Library Way, find a quote on the bronze plaques that means something to you. Why did you choose that quote? What would you write as your own quote?

Book Rec!

Ask a librarian at the Children's Center to recommend a book just for you!

④ ON THE WAY HOME

Thinking It Over

- Why is it important to read books?
- In what ways can scientists use libraries to help them do their jobs?

CAREER FLASH The following careers relate to the New York Public Library. Do you know what each profession does?

- Archivist
- Children's librarian
- Data scientist
- Library page
- Library systems analyst

Pick careers to research. What skills and education are needed to pursue these careers?

NEARBY → GRAND CENTRAL TERMINAL 89 E. 42ND STREET *PAGE 42*
THE NEW VICTORY THEATER 209 W. 42ND STREET *PAGE 140*

NEW YORK TRANSIT MUSEUM

99 Schermerhorn Street, Brooklyn, (718) 694-1600

VISIT: nytransitmuseum.org

ADMISSION

Children *(under 2)*: Free
Children *(2–17)*: $5
Adults: $10
Seniors *(62+)*: $5
Seniors free on Wed.,
except groups

HOURS

TUES.–FRI. 10 AM–4 PM
SAT.–SUN. 11 AM–5 PM

HOW TO GET HERE

Subway: A C F G
R 2 3 4 5

Bus: B25 B26
B38 B41 B45 B52
B54 B57 B61 B62
B63 B65 B67 B103

FOR SPECIAL NEEDS

lslearn.info/nytransmus

SHELLEY REPORTS

All aboard! This place is unbelievable! Located in an old subway station, you'll travel back in time to explore antique trains, vintage buses, turnstiles, tokens, and more!

- **STEEL, STONE, & BACKBONE** Learn about the dedicated workers who built the NYC subway system— their hard work inspired many.

- **MOVING THE MILLIONS** See how subways have changed through the years! Step into 20 vintage subway and elevated cars dating back to 1907.

- **ON THE STREETS** Imagine traveling in trolleys before subways were built underground. Check out traffic lights, parking meters, and interactive "street furniture," too!

- **NOSTALGIA RIDES** On select dates, hop on vintage subway cars and trains and ride to places like Coney Island. It's a blast from the past!

MORE INFO: **ShelleysLearningAdventures.com**

SHELLEY'S ACTIVITIES
NYC Subway and Bus History!

DID YOU KNOW?

There are nine "ghost" subway stations in NYC, which means they're completely abandoned. Spooky!

③ NOW YOU ARE HERE
So Vintage!
In the Moving the Millions area, find your favorite subway car. What do you like about it?

Take the Wheel
Pretend to take a bus out for a spin! Get in the driver's seat and take a picture behind the wheel.

① LET'S GET STARTED
First, visit: nytransitmuseum.org

New Places! New Words!
Look up the definition of these words before you go!

- transit
- trolley
- turnstile
- vintage

② ON THE WAY
Travel Talk
- How did people get around NYC before subways and cars?
- Why do some people prefer traveling in subways instead of cars in NYC?
- Why is it very important that subways run on electricity and not on gas, like cars?

④ ON THE WAY HOME
Thinking It Over
- What challenges were faced by people who built the subway system?
- How would you improve NYC's subways and buses?
- Why is the subway system important to people in NYC?

CAREER FLASH The following careers relate to the New York Transit Museum. Do you know what each profession does?

- Bus driver • Electrical engineer
- Mechanic • Research archivist
- Subway conductor

Pick careers to research. What skills and education are needed to pursue these careers?

9/11 MEMORIAL & MUSEUM

180 Greenwich Street, Manhattan, (212) 266-5211
VISIT: 911memorial.org

MAY WE NEVER FORGET.

MEMORIAL ADMISSION
Free

MUSEUM ADMISSION
Children *(0–6)*: Free
Children *(7–12)*: $15
Young Adults *(13–17)*: $20
Adults: $24

HOURS
Memorial:
DAILY 7:30 AM–9 PM

Museum:
SUN.–THUR. 9 AM–8 PM
FRI.–SAT. 9 AM–9 PM

HOW TO GET HERE
Subway: A C E J
R Z 1 2 3
4 5
Bus: M55 M20 M22

FOR SPECIAL NEEDS
lslearn.info/911mus

SHELLEY REPORTS

This memorial honors the many people killed in the terrorist attacks on the World Trade Center and helps us to understand the significance and impact of this event.

- **9/11 MEMORIAL** Visit this poignant tribute to the tragedy of 9/11. Two giant reflecting pools now rest where the Twin Towers once stood, surrounded by the victims' names carved in bronze. A "Survivor Tree" that endured major damage now continues to grow nearby.

- **HISTORICAL EXHIBITION** Objects and images on display tell the story of 9/11 and its aftermath—pieces of bent steel, a crushed firetruck, and more.

- **DROP-IN ACTIVITY STATIONS** On Saturdays (September–June), participate in remembrance activities like creating 9/11 tribute artwork with red bandana bracelets inspired by a 9/11 hero, and more.

SHELLEY'S ACTIVITIES
Remembering 9/11

DID YOU KNOW?

A team of 350 search and rescue dogs worked up to 16 hours per day searching for victims after the attack.

RESCUE

1 LET'S GET STARTED

First, visit: 911memorial.org

New Places! New Words!

Look up the definition of these words before you go!

- aftermath
- first responder
- memorial
- patriotism

2 ON THE WAY
Travel Talk

- What are the different ways to honor people who have died?
- What is your definition of a hero?
- Why do you think rescue workers put their own lives in danger to help others?

3 NOW YOU ARE HERE
Community

Describe what "community" means to you and your family. Then share a time when you experienced a problem and how you gave or received help from someone in your community.

Reflection

After viewing the 9/11 Memorial, write a poem expressing your feelings or honoring the heroes of 9/11.

4 ON THE WAY HOME
Thinking It Over

- Why is it important to remember what happened on 9/11?
- What is the purpose of the 9/11 Museum, and what did you learn by visiting it?

CAREER FLASH

The following careers relate to the 9/11 Memorial and Museum. Do you know what each profession does?

- Archive digitizer
- Emergency services officer
- Fire captain • Paramedic • Social worker

Pick careers to research. What skills and education are needed to pursue these careers?

NEARBY ➤ NATIONAL MUSEUM OF THE AMERICAN INDIAN ONE BOWLING GREEN *PAGE 82*
SKYSCRAPER MUSEUM 39 BATTERY PLACE *PAGE 116*

101

PELHAM BAY PARK

Watt Avenue & Middletown Road, Bronx, (718) 430-1825

VISIT: nycgovparks.org/parks/pelham-bay-park

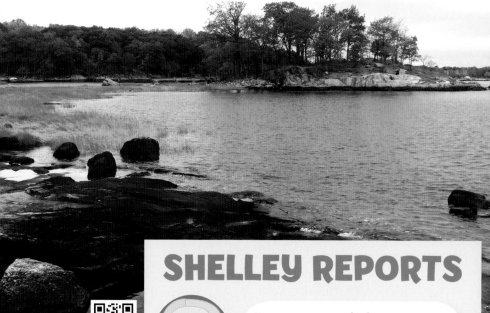

SHELLEY REPORTS

This park is huge! It's the largest public park in New York City! There's tons of room to bike, hike, and explore! It's also a great place to picnic and barbecue!

ADMISSION
Free *
Additional activities' prices vary.

HOURS
Open 24 hours

HOW TO GET HERE
Subway: **6**

Bus: Bx5 Bx12 Bx23, Bx29 Q50
Westchester line 45

FOR SPECIAL NEEDS
lslearn.info/nycparks

- **ADVENTURE AWAITS** Golfing, tennis, fishing, trails—plus Orchard Beach—make Pelham Bay Park a dream for nature and sports lovers!

- **EQUESTRIAN CENTER** Pony and hay-wagon rides offer a chance to explore nature on horseback. How fun!

- **PELHAM BAY NATURE CENTER** Scavenger hunts, nature-inspired crafts and games, and the chance to get up close to animals are all activities offered here.

- **TURTLE COVE GOLF AND BASEBALL** This sports destination offers an 18-hole mini-golf course, batting cages for softball and baseball players, and lessons!

MORE INFO: **ShelleysLearningAdventures.com**

SHELLEY'S ACTIVITIES
Sun and Fun in the Bronx!

DID YOU KNOW?

Orchard Beach is man-made! It was created by covering landfill with barge-loads of white sand!

① LET'S GET STARTED

First, visit: nycgovparks.org/parks/pelham-bay-park

New Places! New Words!

Look up the definition of these words before you go!

- cove
- landfill
- promenade

② ON THE WAY

Travel Talk

- How do people who design playgrounds make sure they're safe for children?
- Why is it rare to see animals other than dogs, pigeons and squirrels in the city?
- In what ways is a nature hike different than going for a walk?

③ NOW YOU ARE HERE

Take a Stroll

Enjoy a mile-long walk along the Orchard Beach promenade and visit playgrounds along the way!

Creature Feature

Take a hike along the trails, then create a field guide with photos and notes of the plants and animals you spotted!

④ ON THE WAY HOME

Thinking It Over

- Why are parks important to people in communities?
- Why is it important to protect the plants and animals on our planet?

CAREER FLASH

The following careers relate to Pelham Bay Park. Do you know what each profession does?

- Botanist • Lifeguard
- Park naturalist
- Sports field maintenance manager
- Structural engineer

What skills and education are needed to pursue these careers?

PREGONES THEATER/PUERTO RICAN TRAVELING THEATER

571 Walton Avenue, Bronx, (718) 585-1202
304 W. 47th Street, Manhattan, (212) 354-1293   VISIT: pregonesprtt.org

SHELLEY REPORTS

ADMISSION
Ticket prices vary by performance. Check the website for discounts, dates, times, and tickets.

HOW TO GET HERE
BRONX
Subway: ② ④ ⑤

Bus: BX1 BX19

MANHATTAN
Subway:
Ⓐ Ⓒ Ⓔ ① ② ③

Bus: M42 M104

FOR SPECIAL NEEDS
Bronx venue is wheelchair accessible. Manhattan venue is not.

¡Fantástico! It's a celebration of Puerto Rican and Latino culture for audiences of all ages. Come celebrate with original bilingual theater and music, from Afro-Dominican to classical.

- **SEASON PERFORMANCES** From Latin jazz, to events celebrating Spanish dances, to comedies, each show explores themes important to Puerto Rican and Latino communities.

- **STAGE GARDEN RUMBA** Combining the talents of amateur and professional artists, these free weekend events use dance, theater, and music to explore environmental themes. Learn more at their website!

- **BX SUMMER BLOCK PARTY!** One day every summer, there's a celebration of Latino music and arts, including performances and showcases featuring the organization's youth talent. Check the calendar for info!

MORE INFO: **ShelleysLearningAdventures.com**

SHELLEY'S ACTIVITIES
Viva el Arte Latino!

DID YOU KNOW?

NYC is home to the largest Puerto Rican population of any city in the world!

③ NOW YOU ARE HERE
Review It!
After the performance, create a video review to share your opinion about the show!

Consider This
In the Bronx theater lobby, check out the gorgeous mural by artist Manny Vega. What does it depict?

① LET'S GET STARTED
First, visit: pregonesprtt.org

New Places! New Words!
Look up the definition of these words before you go!

- *Boricua*
- multimedia
- rumba
- troupe

② ON THE WAY
Travel Talk
- If you owned a theater, what types of performances would you offer?
- How can you communicate with someone who doesn't speak your language?
- Other than holidays, what are some ways a community might celebrate its unique culture?

④ ON THE WAY HOME
Thinking It Over
- What themes or story did the performance explore? How did it make you feel?
- Why should the arts be studied in school?
- How do different types of theater venues influence performances?

CAREER FLASH
The following careers relate to PregonesTheater/ PRTT. Do you know what each profession does?

- Actor • Assistant technical producer
- Film projectionist • Musical director
- Social media manager

Pick careers to research. What skills and education are needed to pursue these careers?

BRONX

MANHATTAN

$$

NEARBY ▶ MANHATTAN: SCIENCE THEATER COMPANY 151 W. 46TH STREET *PAGE 114*
BRONX: THE BRONX MUSEUM OF THE ARTS 1040 GRAND CONCOURSE *PAGE 134*

105

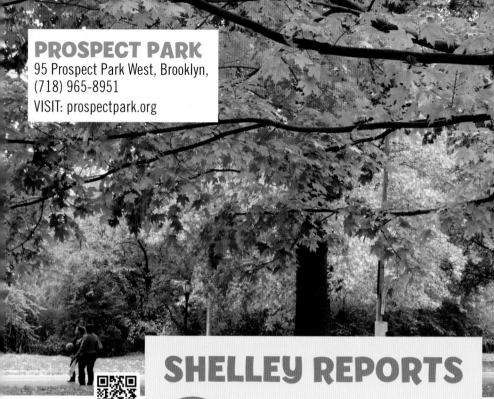

PROSPECT PARK

95 Prospect Park West, Brooklyn,
(718) 965-8951
VISIT: prospectpark.org

ADMISSION
Free
*Additional activities'
prices vary.*

HOURS*
DAILY 5 AM–1 AM
*Hours of attractions vary.
Check website for details.*

HOW TO GET HERE
Subway:  F G Q S
2 3 4 5

Bus: B12 B16 B41
B43 B48 B61 B68

FOR SPECIAL NEEDS
Some paths are
accessible by
wheelchair.

SHELLEY REPORTS

From picnicking and fishing to
birdwatching, ice skating, and
kayaking, there are so many things to
do in this beautiful 585-acre park.

- **LEFRAK CENTER AT LAKESIDE** Enjoy seasonal ice
  and roller skating, boat rentals during summer, and a
  splash pad with more than 20 water jets!

- **PROSPECT PARK ZOO** Here, you can visit otters,
  frogs, and red pandas, as well as unique animals like
  tamarins and cute marmosets!

- **ON THE MOVE** Walk, hike, bike, and enjoy the beauty
  and quiet of this urban oasis.

- **GO FISH!** Bring your own equipment and enjoy
  catch-and-release fishing for largemouth bass,
  bluegill, and pumpkinseed sunfish in Brooklyn's only
  lake! (New York State fishing license required.)

MORE INFO: **ShelleysLearningAdventures.com**

SHELLEY'S ACTIVITIES
Brooklyn's Great Outdoors

DID YOU KNOW?

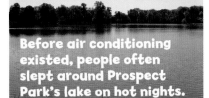

Before air conditioning existed, people often slept around Prospect Park's lake on hot nights.

① LET'S GET STARTED

First, visit: prospectpark.org

New Places! New Words!
Look up the definition of these words before you go!

- esplanade
- pastoral
- pedal boat
- vale

② ON THE WAY
Travel Talk

- How can you learn the age of a tree by carefully looking at its cut stump?

- Compare and contrast ice skating and roller skating. Which would be easier to learn? Why?

- Do you think animals should be kept in zoos? Explain.

③ NOW YOU ARE HERE
Walk It!
With over three miles of paved pathways running around and through the park, it's easy to explore Prospect Park by foot!

On the Water!
Hop in a kayak or pedal boat to see Prospect Park from a new angle—from the center of a lake!

④ ON THE WAY HOME
Thinking It Over

- If you were to design a park as large as this one, what would you include?

- What types of exercise do you enjoy? Where do you do these activities?

CAREER FLASH The following careers relate to Prospect Park. Do you know what each profession does?

- **Forest ecologist** • **Fund-raiser**
- **Groundskeeper** • **Landscape architect**
- **Park administrator**

Pick careers to research. What skills and education are needed to pursue these careers?

QUEENS MUSEUM
Flushing Meadows Corona Park,
Queens, (718) 592-9700
VISIT: queensmuseum.org

SHELLEY REPORTS

Can you find your neighborhood in the Panorama exhibit, a giant model of New York City? Look again and maybe you'll even see your apartment building!

ADMISSION
Suggested Admission:
Children *(under 18)*: Free
Adults: $8
Seniors *(50+)*: $4

HOURS
WED.–SUN
11 AM–5 PM
Closed Mon. and Tues.

HOW TO GET HERE
Subway: **7**

FOR SPECIAL NEEDS
lslearn.info/qnsmuseum

- **NYC PANORAMA** Only here can you tour all of NYC in one room! In this exciting display, check out the mini city, which includes 895,000 buildings.

- **NYC WATER RELIEF MAP** People in NYC use more than one billion gallons of water daily. This giant map shows how it travels into the city. Amazing!

- **WORLD'S FAIR VISIBLE STORAGE** Discover what people in the past dreamed about when they thought about the future at the 1939 and 1964 World's Fairs!

- **SUNDAY FAMILY WORKSHOPS** On Sundays, enjoy art activities, storytelling, and music. It's sure to be fun for all ages!

MORE INFO: **ShelleysLearningAdventures.com**

SHELLEY'S ACTIVITIES
Explore NYC History and More!

DID YOU KNOW?

Surf's up! Surfers can catch a wave at Rockaway Beach in Queens!

① LET'S GET STARTED

First, visit: queensmuseum.org.

New Places! New Words!

Look up the definition of these words before you go!

- borough
- collection
- panorama
- World's Fair

② ON THE WAY

Travel Talk

- Can you name the five boroughs of NYC?
- Name some ways you use water at home. How else might water be used in the city?
- Before the internet and GPS, how do you think people navigated in a city?

③ NOW YOU ARE HERE

NYC Name Game

See who can name the most landmarks at the NYC Panorama!

Wow, You're Strong!

Take a picture pretending to lift up the Unisphere—the giant globe behind the museum.

④ ON THE WAY HOME

Thinking It Over

- Imagine building your own miniature model. What would you build?
- How do you think water was moved through NYC before pipe systems?
- What inventions do you think a World's Fair today would celebrate?

CAREER FLASH

The following careers relate to the Queens Museum. Do you know what each profession does?

- **Archivist**
- **Cartographer**
- **Civil engineer**
- **Model builder**
- **Urban planner**

Pick careers to research. What skills and education are needed to pursue these careers?

NEARBY ▶ LOUIS ARMSTRONG HOUSE MUSEUM 34-56 107TH STREET *PAGE 62*
NEW YORK HALL OF SCIENCE 47-01 111TH STREET *PAGE 92*

QUEENS COUNTY FARM MUSEUM

73-50 Little Neck Parkway, Floral Park, Queens, (718) 347-3276

VISIT: queensfarm.org

ADMISSION

Free

Paid admission during special events. Check website for details.

HOURS

DAILY 10 AM–5 PM

HOW TO GET HERE

Subway: 🄴 🄵

(then transfer to Q46 bus)

Bus: Q36 Q46 QM6

FOR SPECIAL NEEDS

The farm grounds are wheelchair accessible.

SHELLEY REPORTS

Did you know you could visit a real farm right in the city? Dating back to 1697, this 47-acre farm has historic buildings, farm animals, and wonderful special events all year!

- **FEED A GOAT OR SHEEP!** Grab a bag of feed in the gift shop and make friends with the cute animals. They love being petted and fed. Adorable!

- **FARMHOUSE TOUR** On Saturdays and Sundays, get a guided tour of the historic Adriance Farmhouse, a three-room building built in 1772!

- **TAKE A HAYRIDE** From April through October, grab a seat on a giant tractor and take a scenic hayride through the farm. It's bumpy, but fun!

- **FARM STAND** During warmer months, buy fresh fruit, vegetables, and other treats grown on the farm, including delicious eggs from the local hens.

SHELLEY'S ACTIVITIES
Down on the Farm!

DID YOU KNOW?

Nearly one quarter of New York state's land is used for farming.

1 LET'S GET STARTED

First, visit: queensfarm.org

New Places! New Words!
Look up the definition of these words before you go!

- acre
- greenhouse
- orchard
- organic

2 ON THE WAY
Travel Talk

- Where do foods like eggs, milk, and vegetables come from?

- Why are farms important for people everywhere?

- What does it take for a fruit or vegetable to go from a seed to your dinner plate?

3 NOW YOU ARE HERE
Feeding Time!
As you feed the goats and sheep, study their personalities. Are some shy? Are some more excited?

Ask a Farmer
Ask a farmer or guide how a specific vegetable or fruit is grown!

4 ON THE WAY HOME
Thinking It Over

- Why is it important to eat many different types of fruits and vegetables?

- What does the term "farm to table" mean? Why has it become popular?

- How does choosing locally grown produce help the environment?

CAREER FLASH The following careers relate to the Queens County Farm Museum. Do you know what each profession does?

- Agricultural inspector • Egg packer
- Farm manager • Fruit picker
- Veterinarian

What skills and education are needed to pursue these careers?

ROOSEVELT ISLAND
Island between Manhattan and Queens,
(212) 832-4540   VISIT: rioc.ny.gov

ADMISSION
Free*
*Additional activities'
prices vary.

HOW TO GET HERE
Subway: **F**

Bus: Q102 *(to Manhattan tram station)*

Tram: Located at E. 59th Street and 2nd Avenue

Ferry: NYC Ferry to Roosevelt Island, departs E. 34th Street

TRAM HOURS
SUN.–THUR. 6 AM–2 AM
FRI.–SAT. 6 AM–3:30 AM

FOR SPECIAL NEEDS
Tram is wheelchair accessible.

SHELLEY REPORTS

Have you ever been on a tram high above the city? The view is awesome. There are so many amazing historic buildings and parks to explore on this tiny island in the East River.

- **TRAM** For the price of a subway ride, enjoy this thrilling 3-minute journey high above the East River.

- **FDR FOUR FREEDOMS PARK** With stunning waterfront views, this park is a fitting memorial to our 32nd president, Franklin D. Roosevelt—and a wonderful place to enjoy a picnic!

- **RENWICK RUIN** This crumbling, moss-covered gothic revival building was a smallpox hospital in the 1800s and now is an intriguing view into NYC's history.

- **THE LIGHTHOUSE** This historic structure was built in 1872 using rocks from the island. Fascinating!

MORE INFO: **ShelleysLearningAdventures.com**

SHELLEY'S ACTIVITIES
Sky-High Travel & Island Fun!

DID YOU KNOW?

Roosevelt Island is home to NYC's only cat sanctuary— where humans care for around 100 feral cats.

③ NOW YOU ARE HERE
Sky High
On the tram, take a video of the view, narrating what you see! What landmarks can you spot?

Renwick in B&W
Take a color picture of the Renwick Ruin, then add a black-and-white filter. Which version do you like better?

① LET'S GET STARTED
First, visit: rioc.ny.gov

New Places! New Words!
Look up the definition of these words before you go!

- feral
- gothic revival
- smallpox
- tram

② ON THE WAY
Travel Talk

- Who is Roosevelt Island named after?
- Compare and contrast Roosevelt Island with the island of Manhattan.

④ ON THE WAY HOME
Thinking It Over

- How would living on Roosevelt Island be different from living elsewhere in NYC?
- What "four freedoms" did President Roosevelt refer to in his famous speech?

CAREER FLASH The following careers relate to Roosevelt Island. Do you know what each profession does?

- Civil engineer
- Director of parks and recreation
- Memorial sculptor • Tram operator
- Urban planner

Pick careers to research. What skills and education are needed to pursue these careers?

LONG ISLAND CITY TAKE ASTORIA FERRY TO LONG ISLAND CITY *PAGE 60*
MOUNT VERNON HOTEL MUSEUM AND GARDEN 421 E. 61ST STREET *PAGE 66*

113

SCIENCE THEATER COMPANY

The Playroom Theater, 151 W. 46th Street, Manhattan, (212) 967-8278   VISIT: sciencetheatercompany.com

ADMISSION
$60.50

$20 tickets are available 20 minutes before a show begins.

PERFORMANCES
SAT.–SUN.
12 PM AND 3 PM

Visit website to see upcoming show dates and to purchase tickets.

HOW TO GET HERE
Subway: **B D F M**
N R Q W
1 2 7

Bus: BM4 BxM2   M7
M104 M50 M20 M5
Q32 QM1 QM5 QM6

FOR SPECIAL NEEDS
Wheelchair accessible

SHELLEY REPORTS

It looks like magic, but it's really science! You won't believe your eyes when you see these eye-popping, jaw-dropping physics and chemistry experiments, performed live on stage!

- **THAT PHYSICS SHOW** By demonstrating physics principles through extraordinary experiments, this show will have you on the edge of your seat!

- **THAT INVENTIONS SHOW** This new show is presented in association with "The Museum of Interesting Things." Kids will see hands-on demonstrations of cool inventions from the 1850s to the present, and learn how they changed our world!

- **THAT CHEMISTRY SHOW** See a mad scientist prove that science is more unbelievable than magic! Watch exciting science demonstrations such as flames turning green, "elephant toothpaste" overflowing from a giant beaker, and a candle that "drinks" water!

MORE INFO: **ShelleysLearningAdventures.com**

SHELLEY'S ACTIVITIES
Science Magic on Stage!

DID YOU KNOW?

Due to a difference in gravity, a 150-pound person would weigh just 10 pounds on Pluto!

① LET'S GET STARTED

First, visit: sciencetheater company.com

New Places! New Words!

Look up the definition of these words before you go!

- centrifugal force
- gravity
- inertia
- liquid nitrogen
- momentum

② ON THE WAY

Travel Talk

- If there were no gravity on Earth, what would happen?
- How is chemistry involved in baking a cake?
- What happens when you roll a marble up a ramp? What about down the ramp?

③ NOW YOU ARE HERE

Join In

Raise your hand! You might be picked to help with the show on stage.

What's Next?

During each experiment, can you predict what will happen? Call out your prediction when the performer asks you to!

④ ON THE WAY HOME

Thinking It Over

- How are solids, liquids, and gases different?
- Why does a roller coaster designer need to understand physics when creating a ride?
- Would changing the angle of a ramp affect the speed of a marble rolling down it?

CAREER FLASH

The following careers relate to the Science Theater Company. Do you know what each profession does?

- **High school chemistry teacher**
- **Meteorologist • Physicist**
- **Physics demonstrator**
- **Theatrical producer**

What skills and education are needed to pursue these careers?

 NEARBY ➤ **PUERTO RICAN TRAVELING THEATER** 304 W. 47TH STREET *PAGE 104*
THE TOUR AT NBC STUDIOS 30 ROCKEFELLER PLAZA *PAGE 142*

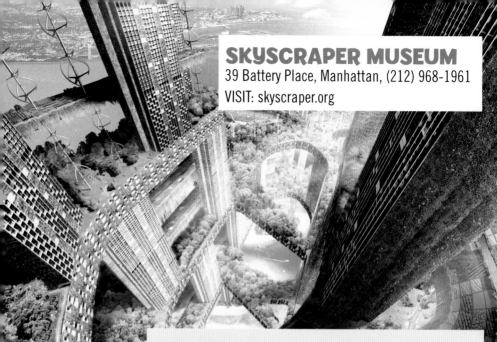

SHELLEY REPORTS

Look! There are huge skyscrapers all around us. Have you ever wondered what inventions helped engineers build such tall buildings? You'll find the answers here.

ADMISSION
Children *(under 12)*: Free
College students: $2.50
Adults: $5
Seniors *(65+)*: $2.50

HOURS
WED.–SUN. 12 PM–6 PM.

HOW TO GET HERE
Subway: ① ④ ⑤ Ⓡ

Bus: M5 M15 M20

FOR SPECIAL NEEDS
Wheelchair accessible

- **WORLD'S TALLEST BUILDINGS: SUPERTALL!**
Get up close to study models of three of the world's tallest skyscrapers. It's so incredible to imagine how they were built.

- **HISTORY OF HEIGHT** This fascinating mural shows how humans have built tall structures for thousands of years—from the pyramids to modern times. It's truly spectacular!

- **TWIN TOWERS EXHIBIT** Explore the history of NYC's famous Twin Towers, from their remarkable construction, to their fate on 9/11, to the rise of One World Trade Center in tribute.

MORE INFO: **ShelleysLearningAdventures.com**

SHELLEY'S ACTIVITIES
Beams, Steel, and Blueprints!

DID YOU KNOW?

In China, it took just 19 days to build one 57-floor skyscraper!

③ NOW YOU ARE HERE

Compare Them!
At the World's Tallest Buildings display, how are the models similar and different?

Historical Heights!
Explore the History of Height mural! When was the shortest structure built? What about the tallest?

① LET'S GET STARTED

First, visit: skyscraper.org

New Places! New Words!
Look up the definition of these words before you go!

- blueprint   • mural
- observation deck
- skyscraper   • steel beam

④ ON THE WAY HOME
Thinking It Over

- What are some challenges of building a skyscraper?
- Describe some skills you'd need to be able to design a skyscraper.
- Which inventions have made building skyscrapers possible?

② ON THE WAY
Travel Talk

- Why do we need to build tall buildings in cities?
- What's your favorite landmark or skyscraper in NYC?

CAREER FLASH

The following careers relate to the Skyscraper Museum. Do you know what each profession does?

- **Civil engineer**
- **Construction site manager**
- **Glazier** • **Steelworker**

Pick careers to research. What skills and education are needed to pursue these careers?

NEARBY ▶ **MUSEUM OF JEWISH HERITAGE** 36 BATTERY PLACE *PAGE 72*
9/11 MEMORIAL & MUSEUM 180 GREENWICH STREET *PAGE 100*

117

SOCRATES SCULPTURE PARK
32-01 Vernon Boulevard, Long Island City, Queens,
(718) 956-1819 x105   VISIT: socratessculpturepark.org

SHELLEY REPORTS

Here you'll find huge, wild, and whimsical art sculptures to touch and explore. It's also a super place for a picnic, with spectacular views of the Manhattan skyline!

ADMISSION
Free

HOURS
DAILY 9 AM—SUNDOWN

HOW TO GET HERE
Subway:

Bus: Q100X Q103
Q104 Q69

Ferry: NYC Ferry to
Astoria Landing

FOR SPECIAL NEEDS
lslearn.info/socpark

- **FREE SCULPTURE WORKSHOPS** On Saturdays from May to September, join visiting artists to paint, glue, and shape materials to create your own sculpted masterpiece!

- **FESTIVALS AND PROGRAMS** The park features family-friendly events all year! Check website.

- **TAKE THE FERRY!** Feel the wind in your hair as the sun warms your skin while taking in the breathtaking NYC vista on this fantastic ride!

MORE INFO: **ShelleysLearningAdventures.com**

SHELLEY'S ACTIVITIES
A Place to Create and Play!

Before becoming a famous Greek philosopher, Socrates was a sculptor!

1 LET'S GET STARTED

First, visit:
socratessculpturepark.org

New Places! New Words!

Look up the definition of these words before you go!

- abstract
- billboard
- conceptual art
- monument

2 ON THE WAY

Travel Talk

- What different materials can be used to create sculptures?
- Are there any sculptures in your home or neighborhood? What do they represent?
- Why do some artists recycle trash to make sculptures?

3 NOW YOU ARE HERE

Deeper Meaning

Find an abstract sculpture while exploring. What do you think the sculpture is about?

Get Up Close!

Feel free to touch the sculptures at the park! Can you tell what they're made of?

4 ON THE WAY HOME

Thinking It Over

- If you could design a sculpture for the park, how would it look?
- Besides creating art for galleries, what other jobs might sculptors be hired to do?

The following careers relate to Socrates Sculpture Park. Do you know what each profession does?

- Director of public programs
- Projection artist
- Sculptor

Pick careers to research. What skills and education are needed to pursue these careers?

NEARBY ▶ MUSEUM OF THE MOVING IMAGE 36-01 35TH AVENUE *PAGE 76*
ROOSEVELT ISLAND ENTER VIA ROOSEVELT ISLAND BRIDGE *PAGE 112*

SOLOMON R. GUGGENHEIM MUSEUM
1071 5th Avenue, Manhattan, (212) 423-3500   VISIT: guggenheim.org

ADMISSION
Children *(under 12)*: Free
Students: $18
Adults: $25
Seniors *(65+)*: $18

HOURS
MON.–WED., FRI., SUN.
10 AM–5:45 PM
SAT. 10 AM–7:45 PM

HOW TO GET HERE
Subway: Q 4 5 6

Bus: M1 M2 M3 M4

FOR SPECIAL NEEDS
lslearn.info/
guggmuseum

SHELLEY REPORTS

Architect Frank Lloyd Wright's huge interior spiral ramp is truly breathtaking, and the perfect way to view the magnificent works of art and sculpture.

- **COOL ARCHITECTURE** From the ground floor of the museum's striking rotunda, admire the gigantic oculus that bathes the museum in natural light. Gorgeous!

- **FAMOUS ARTISTS** Edgar Degas's sculptures, a colorful collection of Picasso's paintings, and stunning works by other artists like Kandinsky and Gauguin are all on display.

- **PROGRAMS FOR CHILDREN** The museum hosts art-making workshops and family-friendly tours! Plus, on weekends, grab a Family Activity Pack at a kiosk for games, self-guided tours, a sketchbook, and more!

MORE INFO: **ShelleysLearningAdventures.com**

SHELLEY'S ACTIVITIES
World-Famous Art and More!

DID YOU KNOW?

Architect Frank Lloyd Wright first planned for the Guggenheim's exterior to be all red instead of white!

3 NOW YOU ARE HERE
What's That?

Some sculptures are very abstract. Without reading the titles, what does each sculpture represent to you?

What Kind of Stairs?

Find the museum's "triangle stairs." Why do you think they received that name?

1 LET'S GET STARTED

First, visit: guggenheim.org

New Places! New Words!

Look up the definition of these words before you go!

- abstract
- avant-garde
- oculus
- modernism

4 ON THE WAY HOME
Thinking It Over

- Compare and contrast the design of the building with other museums you have visited.

- After exploring the museum, which artist's work would you recommend to children your age?

2 ON THE WAY
Travel Talk

- How does an artist know when a piece of art is finished?

- What subjects should an architect study before designing a building?

CAREER FLASH The following careers relate to the Guggenheim Museum. Do you know what each profession does?

- Artist • Digital art conservator
- Director of traveling exhibits
- Photographer • Sculptor
- Structural engineer

What skills and education are needed to pursue these careers?

SPYSCAPE
928 8th Avenue, Manhattan,
(212) 549-1941
VISIT: spyscape.com

ADMISSION
Children *(under 3)*: Free
Children *(3–12)*: $32
Adults *(13+)*: $39
Purchase tickets in advance online to reserve date and time. Check website for VIP ticket prices and information.

HOURS
DAILY 10 AM–8 PM

HOW TO GET HERE
Subway: Ⓐ Ⓑ Ⓒ Ⓓ
Ⓔ Ⓝ Ⓠ Ⓡ Ⓦ

Bus: M7 M20 M104

FOR SPECIAL NEEDS
lslearn.info/spyscape

SHELLEY REPORTS

Do you have what it takes to be a spy? Test your skills at lie detection, surveillance, and dodging lasers at this interactive spy museum. It's a top-secret adventure!

- **SPY HISTORY** Explore the unbelievable stories of world-famous spies, code breakers, and spy catchers! Also check out hidden cameras and other cool gadgets used by real spies.

- **INTERACTIVE EXPERIENCE** Time to pretend you're Bond . . . James Bond. Climb and dart around moving lasers, then experience interrogation and surveillance firsthand. Intense!

- **SPY PROFILE** A hacker, cryptologist, or a spycatcher? Complete thrilling tasks of espionage to find out what type of spy you should be.

MORE INFO: **ShelleysLearningAdventures.com**

SHELLEY'S ACTIVITIES
I SPY!

DID YOU KNOW?

George Washington used invisible ink to write top secret messages during the Revolutionary War (1775-1783).

3 NOW YOU ARE HERE

Spy Job!

Find out your suggested spy career through the Spy Profile! Do you agree with the recommendation? Why?

Pay Attention!

After you leave the video surveillance room, what details can you remember from the scenes?

1 LET'S GET STARTED

First, visit: spyscape.com

New Places! New Words!

Look up the definition of these words before you go!

- espionage
- interrogation
- lie-detector
- surveillance

4 ON THE WAY HOME

Thinking It Over

- How is being a spy a scary or difficult job? How is it fun?
- List synonyms for the word "spy."
- Why do spies need to be good at keeping secrets?

2 ON THE WAY

Travel Talk

- Why do governments use spies to collect information?
- How do spies gather information without others finding out who they are?
- Who are some famous spies in movies, cartoons, and games?

 CAREER FLASH The following careers relate to Spyscape. Do you know what each profession does?

- **A/V technician**
- **Computer forensic examiner**
- **Cyber threat analyst**
- **Digital encryption expert** • **Field agent**
- **Director of security**

What skills and education are needed to pursue these careers?

NEARBY **FDNY FIRE ZONE** ROCKEFELLER CENTER, 34 W. 51ST STREET *PAGE 34*
THE TOUR AT NBC STUDIOS 30 ROCKEFELLER PLAZA *PAGE 142*

STATEN ISLAND CHILDREN'S MUSEUM

1000 Richmond Terrace, Staten Island, (718) 273-2060
VISIT: sichildrensmuseum.org

ADMISSION
Children *(under 1)*: Free
General admission: $8*
*Free admission Wed.,
3 PM–5 PM*

HOURS
TUES.–FRI. 11 AM–5 PM
SAT.–SUN. 10 AM–5 PM

HOW TO GET HERE
Subway:

🄹 🅁 🅉 ① ④ ⑤

to Staten Island Ferry
terminal, then tranfer to
S40 bus

Bus: S40 S44

FOR SPECIAL NEEDS
lslearn.info/
sichildmuseum

SHELLEY REPORTS

Prepare to jam with the insect orchestra or even build an igloo! Enjoy creative hands-on interactive activities designed to celebrate many different learning styles.

- **BUGS!** Get a close-up view of cockroaches, pinktoe tarantulas, truly magnificent millipedes, and sometimes even bees building a hive!

- **HOUSE ABOUT IT** Grab a real drill, use a digger, and knock over blocks with a wrecking ball to learn how houses are built.

- **GREAT EXPLORATIONS** Experience environments such as the Arctic tundra, the deep sea, and a rain forest canopy through fun hands-on activities.

- **HISTORIC BUILDINGS** Visit Snug Harbor's structures, built to look like Greek temples. Can you spot towering columns and other neat Greek building details?

MORE INFO: **ShelleysLearningAdventures.com**

SHELLEY'S ACTIVITIES
Hands-On Fun in Staten Island!

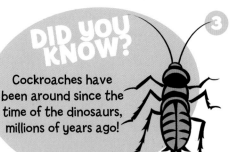

DID YOU KNOW?

Cockroaches have been around since the time of the dinosaurs, millions of years ago!

1 LET'S GET STARTED

First, visit: sichildrensmuseum.org

New Places! New Words!
Look up the definition of these words before you go!

- arthropod
- millipede
- pollination
- rain forest canopy

2 ON THE WAY
Travel Talk

- What would happen to the environment if insects disappeared forever?
- What is pollination, and why is it an important part of our planet's ecosystems?

3 NOW YOU ARE HERE
Green Thumb Fun!
At the Garden Terrace, plant flowers, paint with water, and help grow plants to feed the museum's bugs!

Firefighter-in-Training!
At Ladder 11, hop aboard a real 1941 fire truck, slide down a fire pole, and try on real firefighting gear!

4 ON THE WAY HOME
Thinking It Over

- How do honeybees help humans and the environment?
- What math and science skills do construction workers use when building a new house?

CAREER FLASH

The following careers relate to the Staten Island Children's Museum. Do you know what each profession does?

- Arachnologist
- Construction contractor
- Construction equipment operator
- Visual arts teacher

What skills and education are needed to pursue these careers?

ADMISSION*
Children *(under 3)*: Free
Children *(4–12)*: $9
Adults: $18.50
Seniors *(62+)*: $14
Includes admission to Ellis Island and Liberty Island grounds.

HOURS
Manhattan Ferry Daily Departures
8:30 AM–5 PM

HOW TO GET HERE
Manhattan Ferry
(Castle Clinton at Battery Park):

Subway:
R W 1 4 5

Bus: M1 M6 M15

FOR SPECIAL NEEDS
lslearn.info/statliberty

SHELLEY REPORTS

After a long, hard overseas journey, many immigrants cried when they first saw this statue. Lady Liberty continues to symbolize hope and freedom to people everywhere.

- **PARK RANGER TOUR** Meet at the flagpole for a free grounds tour, led by a park ranger. Discover the history of the statue, what it represents to people around the world, and more! (Hourly tours)

- **PEDESTAL AND MUSEUM** At the museum, check out a replica of the statue's face and foot, her original torch, and artifacts that tell the inspiring story of Lady Liberty. (Must have a Pedestal ticket.)

- **CLIMB TO THE CROWN** Scale the stairs to reach the incredible view from the crown! Inside, glimpse at the statue's impressive inner structure. (Must have a Crown ticket.)

MORE INFO: **ShelleysLearningAdventures.com**

SHELLEY'S ACTIVITIES
Get Up Close to Lady Liberty!

DID YOU KNOW?

The seven spikes on the Statue of Liberty's crown are believed to symbolize Earth's seven continents and seas.

③ NOW YOU ARE HERE
Ranger Time!

At the Liberty Island info center, get a booklet, pencil, and directions from rangers and try to earn a Junior Ranger badge!

Liberty for All!

Many parts of Lady Liberty's design symbolize freedom and liberty. Can you identify them? Ask a park ranger for assistance!

① LET'S GET STARTED

First, visit: statuecruises.com

New Places! New Words!

Look up the definition of these words before you go!

- colossus
- enlightenment
- liberty
- oxidation

④ ON THE WAY HOME
Thinking It Over

- The statue's official title is Liberty Enlightening the World. What does that mean?
- What do the broken chains around Lady Liberty's feet symbolize?

② ON THE WAY
Travel Talk

- The Statue is sometimes called the "Mother of Exiles." What does that mean?
- What freedoms do we have in the US that aren't available in some other countries?

CAREER FLASH

The following careers relate to the Statue of Liberty. Do you know what each profession does?

- **Director of marketing**
- **Park ranger**
- **Port captain**
- **Statue restoration project manager**

What skills and education are needed to pursue these careers?

SUGAR HILL CHILDREN'S MUSEUM OF ART AND STORYTELLING

898 St. Nicholas Avenue, Manhattan, (212) 335-0004

VISIT: sugarhillmuseum.org

SHELLEY REPORTS

Explore cool, colorful art exhibitions and a studio lab where you'll create your own masterpieces. And don't forget to check out the wonderful storytelling workshops.

ADMISSION
Children *(under 9)*: Free
Children *(9–17)*: $4
Students *(with ID)*: $4
Adults: $7
Seniors *(65+)*: $4

HOURS
THUR.–SUN.
10 AM–5 PM

HOW TO GET HERE
Subway:

Bus: Bx6 M2 M3
M100 M101

FOR SPECIAL NEEDS
lslearn.info/sughill

- **ART EXHIBITIONS** The colorful and vibrant art is often inspired by Harlem's Sugar Hill neighborhood and explores themes that are meaningful to the community.

- **STUDIO LAB** Collaborate with others and experiment with different tools and materials to create your own fabulous works of art.

- **STORY HOUR** Visiting storytellers use art, dance, and movement to tell exciting tales. These stories will take you to imaginary worlds both near and far!

- **READING NOOK** In this special corner of the museum, you can pick a book, get cozy, and get lost in the pages for as long as you wish.

MORE INFO: **ShelleysLearningAdventures.com**

SHELLEY'S ACTIVITIES
Art and Storytelling Fun!

DID YOU KNOW?

Sugar Hill is a Harlem neighborhood with a rich history. African Americans who have lived there include composer Duke Ellington and Justice Thurgood Marshall.

③ NOW YOU ARE HERE
What's the Story?

In the Reading Nook, choose a book to read. What was it about that book that caught your eye?

Make a Picture

At the Studio Lab, create a piece of art, then take a picture of it!

① LET'S GET STARTED

First, visit: sugarhillmuseum.org

New Places! New Words!

Look up the definition of these words before you go!

- artist in residence
- collaboration
- community
- self-expression

② ON THE WAY
Travel Talk

- Describe what makes a story interesting to readers.
- Do you have a favorite story? Why do you like it?
- What would you include in a story about your neighborhood?

④ ON THE WAY HOME
Thinking It Over

- How might an artist choose what to create?
- What is one interesting thing you learned about the Sugar Hill neighborhood?
- Why do children's books often use rhyme and pictures to help tell stories?

CAREER FLASH The following careers relate to the Sugar Hill Children's Museum. Do you know what each profession does?

- **Book illustrator** • **Literary agent** • **Writer**

Pick careers to research. What skills and education are needed to pursue these careers?

NEARBY ➤ UNITED PALACE 4140 BROADWAY *PAGE 146*

TEATRO SEA

107 Suffolk Street, Suite 202,
Manhattan, (212) 529-1545
VISIT: teatrosea.org

SHELLEY REPORTS

This cozy bilingual Latino theater features performances of folk stories and fairy tales in English and Spanish!

ADMISSION
Ticket prices vary depending on show.

HOURS
Visit teatrosea.org for more info about show dates, times, and costs.

HOW TO GET HERE
Subway: F J M Z

Bus:
M9 M14A B39 M21

FOR SPECIAL NEEDS:
Wheelchair accessible

- **BILINGUAL PERFORMANCES** Child-friendly shows entertain in two languages—each musical and play is performed in English and Spanish! *Te va a encantar!*

- **LITTLE PUPPET MUSEUM** Puppets have been used for thousands of years in every culture to tell stories. Meet the hundreds of cool puppets on display!

- **COMMUNITY PROGRAMS** Check out the Teatro SEA website for unique family events offered all year! They feature a variety of programs celebrating Latino artists.

- **LATINIZED CLASSICS** From Little Red Riding Hood to the Three Little Pigs, familiar fairy tale heroes are the stars of many shows—all with a Latin twist. Check the calendar!

MORE INFO: **ShelleysLearningAdventures.com**

SHELLEY'S ACTIVITIES
Bilingual Theater Fun!

DID YOU KNOW?

Shadow puppetry is an ancient form of storytelling first used in India, China, and many other cultures long ago.

1 LET'S GET STARTED

First, visit: teatrosea.org

New Places! New Words!
Look up the definition of these words before you go!

- bilingual
- folk tale
- marionette
- repertory

2 ON THE WAY
Travel Talk

- What puppets have you seen on TV or in the movies?
- If you were in a play, would you rather perform on stage or help out behind the scenes?
- What are the advantages of learning a second language?

3 NOW YOU ARE HERE
Story Time!
In the Little Puppet Museum, pick out your favorite puppet and create a story about it.

What Did You Learn?
After the show, discuss what you learned from the performance.

4 ON THE WAY HOME
Thinking It Over

- Why do you think some plays use puppets instead of costumed actors?
- Compare and contrast different types of puppetry.
- How did some characters show how they were feeling without using words?

CAREER FLASH The following careers relate to experiencing Teatro SEA. Do you know what each profession does?

- **Box office salesperson** • **Playwright**
- **Puppeteer** • **Show producer**
- **Translator**

Pick careers to research. What skills and education are needed to pursue these careers?

NEARBY MUSEUM OF CHINESE IN AMERICA 215 CENTRE STREET *PAGE 68*
TENEMENT MUSEUM 103 ORCHARD STREET *PAGE 132*

TENEMENT MUSEUM

103 Orchard Street, Manhattan,
(877) 975-3786   VISIT: tenement.org

ADMISSION
Children *(6–17)*: $20
Adults: $25
Seniors *(65+)*: $20

HOURS
FRI.–WED.
10 AM–6:30 PM,
THUR.
10 AM–8:30 PM
Closed Mon. and Tues.

Reserve tickets online
or by phone.

HOW TO GET HERE
Subway: B D F
J M Z

Bus: M15

FOR SPECIAL NEEDS:
lslearn.info/tenmuse

SHELLEY REPORTS

Take a step back in time to tour
apartments from long ago and
explore the lives of immigrants
who lived in the Lower East Side.

- **TOUR THE APARTMENTS** Step back in time and
experience how NYC immigrants lived more than
100 years ago.

- **MEET THE RESIDENTS** Wouldn't it be cool to talk
to someone from the 1800s or early 1900s? Here,
actors playing immigrants answer questions about
life back then! Call to confirm event.

- **WALKING TOURS** Experience the Lower East Side
through the eyes of immigrants who helped build the
neighborhood. It's like traveling in a time machine!

- **MEET THE NEW IMMIGRANTS** Learn about the
Chinese and Puerto Rican immigrants who helped
redefine NYC from the 1950s through the 1970s.

MORE INFO: **ShelleysLearningAdventures.com**

SHELLEY'S ACTIVITIES
Explore NYC Life Long Ago!

DID YOU KNOW?

One hundred years ago, children didn't have video games. They often played games with tops and marbles instead!

① LET'S GET STARTED

First, visit: tenement.org.

New Places! New Words!

Look up the definition of these words before you go!

- immigrant
- oral history
- sweatshop
- tenement

② ON THE WAY
Travel Talk

- Can you name something historians might study to learn about the past?

- What would someone from the future learn about you if they studied your home?

- How do diaries and letters help people understand the past?

③ NOW YOU ARE HERE
Family Photo!

Take a few pics while touring the museum—it's history in the making!

"I Spy"

Take turns playing "I Spy" to identify historical items you see on the tours.

④ ON THE WAY HOME
Thinking It Over

- In the 1800s, how do you think life was different for children in NYC?

- If you could live in the early 1900s for a week, would you do it?

- What objects in your home would someone from the 1960s not be able to recognize?

CAREER FLASH

The following careers relate to the Tenement Museum and its tours. Do you know what each profession does?

- **Actor**
- **American Sign Language interpreter**
- **Archive technician**
- **Gift shop manager** • **Historian**

Pick careers to research. What skills and education are needed to pursue these careers?

NEARBY ▶ MUSEUM OF CHINESE IN AMERICA 215 CENTRE STREET *PAGE 68*
TEATRO SEA 107 SUFFOLK STREET, SUITE 202 *PAGE 130*

THE BRONX MUSEUM OF THE ARTS

1040 Grand Concourse, Bronx, (718) 681-6000   VISIT: bronxmuseum.org

SHELLEY REPORTS

The Bronx has amazing artists! You'll see the creations of local artists and others to honor the borough's rich diversity.

ADMISSION
Free

HOURS
WED. 1 PM–6 PM
THUR., SAT., AND SUN.
11AM–6 PM
FRI. 11AM–8 PM
Closed Mon. and Tues.

HOW TO GET HERE
Subway:

Bus: Bx1 Bx2 BxM4

FOR SPECIAL NEEDS
lslearn.info/bxmuseart

- **EXHIBITS GALORE!** Using artwork, photos, video, and sculptures, exhibits often tell a powerful story of what life is like in the Bronx.

- **LOCAL ARTISTS** The museum's exhibits celebrate artists from the Bronx while highlighting themes like community life and diversity. They're sure to challenge and inspire you!

- **FAMILY AFFAIR** Get ready! On some Saturdays, the museum offers terrific activities for children to do with their parents or guardians, like art-making. Check the calendar!

MORE INFO: **ShelleysLearningAdventures.com**

SHELLEY'S ACTIVITIES
Explore Art in the Bronx!

DID YOU KNOW?

In 1919, six brothers living in the Bronx carved the statue for the Lincoln Memorial, located in Washington, DC.

① LET'S GET STARTED

First, visit: bronxmuseum.org.

New Places! New Words!
Look up the definition of these words before you go!

- community
- contemporary art
- mural • diversity

② ON THE WAY
Travel Talk

- Imagine a piece of art about your neighborhood. What would it look like?
- What might inspire artists to create art?
- Picture yourself as an artist! What type of artist would you be and why?

③ NOW YOU ARE HERE
Art and Emotion
Find your favorite artwork at the museum. How does it make you feel?

Tell a Story!
Pick out a piece of art about the Bronx. Can you tell a story about what it represents?

④ ON THE WAY HOME
Thinking It Over

- Why do visual artists use images and colors to tell a story instead of words?
- What did you learn about the Bronx after viewing the artwork?

CAREER FLASH

The following jobs help support museums. Do you know what each profession does?

- **Art conservator • Event planner**
- **Public relations manager**
- **Sculptor • Social media manager**

Pick jobs to research. What skills and education are needed to pursue these careers?

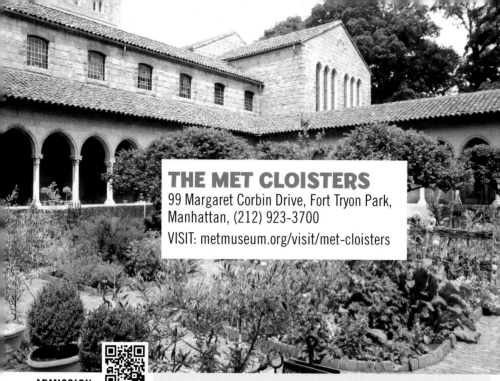

THE MET CLOISTERS

99 Margaret Corbin Drive, Fort Tryon Park, Manhattan, (212) 923-3700

VISIT: metmuseum.org/visit/met-cloisters

ADMISSION

New York State residents: Pay what you wish.

Visitors from outside NY:
Children *(under 12)*: Free
Students: $12
Adults: $25
Seniors *(65+)*: $17

HOURS

MAR.–OCT.
10 AM–5:15 PM
NOV.–FEB.
10 AM–4:45 PM

HOW TO GET HERE

Subway: **A**

Bus: M4

FOR SPECIAL NEEDS

lslearn.info/cloisters

SHELLEY REPORTS

Calling all kings and queens! This magical uptown museum looks just like a castle. There are breathtaking gardens and views of the Hudson River.

- **THE GARDENS** Walk through these gardens brimming with plants that were typically grown in medieval times—including a variety of flowers, herbs, and medicinals.

- **ART** As seen in the *Harry Potter* films, the Met Cloisters' set of Unicorn Tapestries are among the famous medieval art pieces on display. How special!

- **STAINED GLASS** Check out the brightly colored scenes of angels, queens, and more depicted in the stained glass on display here. They're dazzling!

SHELLEY'S ACTIVITIES
Enjoy Medieval Art and History!

DID YOU KNOW?

In 1363, King Edward III made it a law that all men had to practice archery two hours a week!

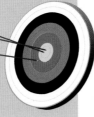

① LET'S GET STARTED

First, visit: metmuseum.org/visit/met-cloisters

New Places! New Words!

Look up the definition of these words before you go!

- cloister
- coat of arms
- medieval
- Middle Ages
- tapestry

② ON THE WAY
Travel Talk

- Do you think living in medieval times was more difficult than living today? Explain.
- How would life in a castle differ from life in a house or apartment?
- What can we learn from studying artwork made long ago?

③ NOW YOU ARE HERE
Mythical Meanings

Study the seven Unicorn Tapestries. Why were they created? Describe what features you like best.

Create a Coat

Imagine a coat of arms for your family. What animals or symbols would it include? Sketch it!

④ ON THE WAY HOME
Thinking It Over

- What was education like for children during medieval times?
- During medieval times, why did people use plants as medicine?

CAREER FLASH The following careers relate to the Met Cloisters. Do you know what each profession does?

- Curator of medieval arts
- Email program manager
- Horticultural researcher
- Medieval historian
- Restoration architect • Stonemason

Pick careers to research. What skills and education are needed to pursue these careers?

NEARBY UNITED PALACE 4140 BROADWAY *PAGE 146*

THE MUSEUM AT FASHION INSTITUTE OF TECHNOLOGY

Seventh Avenue at 27th Street, Manhattan,
(212) 217-4558   VISIT: fitnyc.edu/museum

SHELLEY REPORTS

> If you like fashion, you'll love this place. Learn how technology is used to make the latest styles and discover amazing clothing and accessories from the past.

ADMISSION
Free

HOURS
TUES.–FRI. 12 PM–8 PM
SAT. 10 AM–5 PM
Closed Sun. and Mon.

HOW TO GET HERE
Subway: Ⓐ Ⓒ Ⓔ Ⓕ
Ⓜ Ⓝ Ⓡ ①

Bus: M20 M23 M34

FOR SPECIAL NEEDS
lslearn.info/fitmuseum

- **SPECIAL EXHIBITIONS** View clothing inspired by everything from nature, to fairy tales, to sports. These exhibits change often—you never know what you'll see!

- **THE FASHION AND TEXTILE HISTORY GALLERY** This exhibit showcases a changing display of fascinating fashion—past items range from red wedding dresses to outer space–themed pantsuits!

- **GALLERY FIT** This gallery celebrates the creativity of FIT students and teachers. The bright future of fashion design starts here!

- **INCREDIBLE ACCESSORIES** The museum's exhibits draw from a breathtaking collection of hats, shoes, fans, and costume jewelry created by world-famous designers.

SHELLEY'S ACTIVITIES
See Fashion through the Ages!

DID YOU KNOW?

In the 1300s, men liked wearing long-toed shoes. Some shoes were 24 inches long!

③ NOW YOU ARE HERE
Spot a Rainbow!
Can you find every color in the rainbow in the museum's different exhibits?

Who Wore This?
Pick a garment on display that interests you. Make up a story about the person who wore it.

① LET'S GET STARTED
First, visit: fitnyc.edu/museum

New Places! New Words!
Look up the definition of these words before you go!

- accessory
- costume jewelry
- garment
- pattern

② ON THE WAY
Travel Talk

- What is your favorite thing to wear? Why do you like it?
- What steps might a fashion designer take to create a new dress?
- Have you ever wondered how fabrics get their colors or patterns?

④ ON THE WAY HOME
Thinking It Over

- What was your favorite piece of clothing at the museum? Why?
- If you designed a garment to display at the Museum, what would it be?
- Pick an item of clothing that technology could improve. Describe it.

CAREER FLASH

The following careers are in the fashion industry. Do you know what each profession does?

- **Color technologist**
- **Costume designer**
- **Fashion photographer**
- **Fashion publicist**
- **Textile designer**

What skills and education are needed to pursue these careers?

NEARBY ▶

JAZZ STANDARD YOUTH ORCHESTRA 116 E. 27TH STREET *PAGE 54*
NATIONAL MUSEUM OF MATHEMATICS 11 E. 26TH STREET *PAGE 80*

THE NEW VICTORY THEATER
209 W. 42nd Street, Manhattan, (646) 223-3010   VISIT: newvictory.org

ADMISSION
Ticket prices vary by performance. Check website for details.

HOURS
Visit website to review performance descriptions, dates, showtimes, and to purchase tickets.

HOW TO GET HERE
Subway:
Ⓐ Ⓒ Ⓔ Ⓝ Ⓠ Ⓡ Ⓢ Ⓦ ① ② ③ ⑦

Bus: M7 M20 M34A M42 M104

FOR SPECIAL NEEDS
lslearn.info/newvic

SHELLEY REPORTS

Experience exciting and unique performances from around the world in the heart of Times Square. From African drumming to juggling, who knows what you'll see and hear!

- **ALL KINDS OF SHOWS!** Puppetry, Shakespeare, acrobatics, and opera—oh my! There are countless ways to be entertained at the New Victory. Every show dazzles!

- **FAMILY ENGAGEMENT** Get ready to laugh, jump, draw, and dance before and after performances as teaching artists lead creative play activities. Super fun!

- **AUTISM-FRIENDLY PERFORMANCES** Several times a year, the New Victory creates performances for children with autism. From the lights to the sounds, every detail makes all feel welcome.

MORE INFO: **ShelleysLearningAdventures.com**

SHELLEY'S ACTIVITIES
NYC's Family-Friendly Theater!

DID YOU KNOW?

Times Square is so bright, it's one of the few places that astronauts can identify from outer space!

③ NOW YOU ARE HERE
Play Together!
Say hi to an on-site teaching artist. Have them show you a fun art activity!

Instagram This
Share a photo of yourself standing under the marquee outside the theater!

① LET'S GET STARTED
First, visit: newvictory.org

New Places! New Words!
Look up the definition of these words before you go!

- acrobatics
- marquee
- opera
- performing arts
- production

② ON THE WAY
Travel Talk

- How might someone perform on stage without using words?
- Would you rather watch a play or perform in one? Why?
- Who is your favorite character in a story? Why do you like them?

④ ON THE WAY HOME
Thinking It Over

- Why are theaters important to people and communities?
- Imagine creating a play for the New Victory Theater. What would it be about?
- How is seeing a live performance more fun than watching a performance on TV?

CAREER FLASH — The following careers relate to the New Victory Theater. Do you know what each profession does?

- Choreographer
- Scenic carpenter
- Stage manager
- UI/UX engineer

Pick jobs to research. What skills and education are needed to pursue these careers?

NEARBY → GULLIVER'S GATE 216 W. 44TH STREET *PAGE 44*
NATIONAL GEOGRAPHIC ENCOUNTER: OCEAN ODYSSEY 226 W. 44TH STREET *PAGE 78*

THE TOUR AT NBC STUDIOS

30 Rockefeller Plaza, Manhattan, (212) 664-3700

VISIT: thetouratnbcstudios.com

ADMISSION
Children *(6–12)**: $29
Adults: $33
Seniors *(55+)*: $29
*No children under 6.

HOURS*
MON.–THUR.
8:20 AM–2:20 PM
FRI. 8:20 AM–5:00 PM
SELECT SAT.–SUN.
8:20 AM–6:00 PM
*Tours depart every 20 minutes, book online.

HOW TO GET HERE
Subway: B D F M
N Q R 1 6

Bus: M1 M2 M3 M4
M5 M7 M50

FOR SPECIAL NEEDS
lslearn.info/nbcstudios

SHELLEY REPORTS

Lights, camera, action! Get behind the scenes and visit real TV studios where your favorite shows are made! You'll learn about TV production and the people who make it happen!

- **STUDIO TOUR** Explore the magic of TV! Join an NBC page on a backstage tour of shows like *Saturday Night Live* or *The Tonight Show Starring Jimmy Fallon.*

- **CREATE YOUR OWN SHOW** Tape your own version of a talk show! Try your hand in the hosting chair, as a guest, or as part of the band—then download your show for an incredible souvenir!

- **ART AND ARCHITECTURE** Experience towering art deco buildings, colorful mosaics, and giant murals in historic Rockefeller Center. And don't forget to visit the beautiful outdoor gardens and the ice rink in the winter. It's all truly captivating!

MORE INFO: **ShelleysLearningAdventures.com**

SHELLEY'S ACTIVITIES
The Magic of Television

DID YOU KNOW?

A comedian is often used to warm up a live TV audience with jokes before the show begins—getting them ready to laugh on air!

① LET'S GET STARTED

First, visit:
thetouratnbcstudios.com

New Places! New Words!

Look up the definition of these words before you go!

- broadcast
- live-action
- monologue
- page

② ON THE WAY

Travel Talk

- Besides actors, what other jobs are needed on set to create a TV show?

- Why might a TV show be shot in a studio instead of at a real-life location?

- If you made a TV show, what would it be about? Would it be animated or live-action?

③ NOW YOU ARE HERE

You Be the Judge!

In the Shop at NBC Studios, take a seat in one of *The Voice's* famous judges' chairs for an unforgettable photo op!

Name That Flag!

Outside 30 Rock, look up at the 200 country flags standing tall in the plaza. How many countries' flags can you identify?

④ ON THE WAY HOME

Thinking It Over

- What qualities does an NBC page need to give a successful studio tour?

- If you could work on a TV show, would you want to be behind the scenes or on stage? Why?

CAREER FLASH The following careers relate to the Tour at NBC Studios. Do you know what each profession does?

- Camera operator
- NBC page
- Scriptwriter
- Studio technician
- TV production assistant

Pick careers to research. What skills and education are needed to pursue these careers?

NEARBY ▶ FDNY FIRE ZONE ROCKEFELLER CENTER, 34 W. 51ST STREET *PAGE 34*
SCIENCE THEATER COMPANY, THE PLAYROOM THEATER 151 W. 46TH STREET *PAGE 114*

UNITED NATIONS
405 E. 42nd Street, Manhattan,
(212) 963-4475   VISIT: visit.un.org

ADMISSION

Children *(5–12)*: $13
Students *(13+)*: $15
Adults: $22
Seniors *(60+)*: $13

HOURS

DAILY 9 AM–4:45 PM
Guided tours Mon.–Fri.

HOW TO GET HERE

Subway:
S 4 5 6 7

Bus: M15 M42 M101
M102 M103 Q32

FOR SPECIAL NEEDS

lslearn.info/un

SHELLEY REPORTS

Yes, you can really help people around the world! Visit the UN to learn how nations come together to solve problems that improve people's lives on every continent.

- **MAIN TOUR** Learn how the UN works on issues like world peace and human rights in the General Assembly Hall, the Security Council Chamber, and other important UN gathering places. (Ages 5+)

- **UN CHILDREN'S TOUR** See wall-sized world maps, a full-size refugee tent, and learn about how the UN is helping children in need around the world. (Ages 5–10, tour offered daily at 3:50 PM)

- **UNICEF DANNY KAYE VISITORS CENTRE** Located across the street from the UN, exhibits feature UNICEF'S powerful history of helping children around the globe.

MORE INFO: **ShelleysLearningAdventures.com**

SHELLEY'S ACTIVITIES
Helping Others around the World!

DID YOU KNOW?

The UN has its own post office, and even issues its own postage stamps!

① LET'S GET STARTED

First, visit: visit.un.org

New Places! New Words!

Look up the definition of these words before you go!

- delegation
- human rights
- member states
- refugee

② ON THE WAY

Travel Talk

- What human rights do you think every person around the world should receive?
- Name some things that all children around the world need in order to stay healthy and grow strong.

③ NOW YOU ARE HERE

Interactive Games!

During the UN Kids' Tour, play interactive games and do quizzes with the tour guides!

Visit the Visitor's Center!

Stop by the Visitor's Center for free brochures, fact sheets, and posters to learn more about the United Nations.

④ ON THE WAY HOME

Thinking It Over

- After your visit, can you name some ways the UN helps people in need?
- Why is it important for nations to have a central organization like the UN to help solve problems?

CAREER FLASH

The following careers relate to the United Nations. Do you know what each profession does?

- Diplomat • Economic advisor
- Human rights officer • Software engineer
- Spokesperson

Pick careers to research. What skills and education are needed to pursue these careers?

UNITED PALACE
4140 Broadway, Manhattan, (212) 568-6700
VISIT: unitedpalace.org

ADMISSION
Some events free with RSVP. Child rates not available for some performances. Check website for prices, dates, show times, and tickets.

HOW TO GET HERE
Subway: Ⓐ ①

Bus: M3 M4 M5 M7 M100 BX3 BX11 BX13 BX35 BX36

FOR SPECIAL NEEDS
Wheelchair accessible

SHELLEY REPORTS

This theater is glamorous and spectacular! It's the perfect place to see a movie or a live performance. Don't forget to take a tour to learn all about its fabulous history.

- **TOURS** Explore the mezzanine, grand foyer, and balconies of this historic theater and marvel at its lavish decorations.

- **PERFORMANCES AND MOVIES** With its soaring golden columns and ornate ceiling, you're unlikely to find a more magical place to see a performance or a film!

- **LOBBY SERIES** On Monday nights, the United Palace's stunning, gilded foyer is a dazzling place to watch up-and-coming musicians, dancers, and artists!

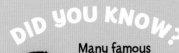

SHELLEY'S ACTIVITIES
Step into a Grand Theater!

DID YOU KNOW?

Many famous musical acts have performed at the United Palace, including Bob Dylan, Adele, and John Legend.

① LET'S GET STARTED

First, visit: unitedpalace.org

New Places! New Words!

Look up the definition of these words before you go!

- foyer
- gilded
- Jazz Age
- mezzanine

② ON THE WAY
Travel Talk

- Which type of entertainment do you like best—a movie, a play, or a concert?
- How does the design of a theater influence the experience of seeing a performance or movie?

③ NOW YOU ARE HERE
Hidden Objects

Look closely at the decorated walls and columns in the lobby and mezzanine. What animals and people do you see?

How Quotable!

Read the Rev. Ike quotes on the lobby walls. Which one do you like best?

④ ON THE WAY HOME
Thinking It Over

- How are movie theaters today different from the United Palace?
- Why are people interested in restoring old, historic buildings?
- If you designed a theater, what would it look like?

CAREER FLASH

The following careers relate to the United Palace. Do you know what each profession does?

- Actor • Audio engineer
- Film projectionist • Hip-hop choreographer
- Restoration architect

Pick careers to research. What skills and education are needed to pursue these careers?

NEARBY ➡ SUGAR HILL CHILDREN'S MUSEUM 898 ST. NICHOLAS AVENUE *PAGE 128*
THE MET CLOISTERS 99 MARGARET CORBIN DRIVE *PAGE 136*

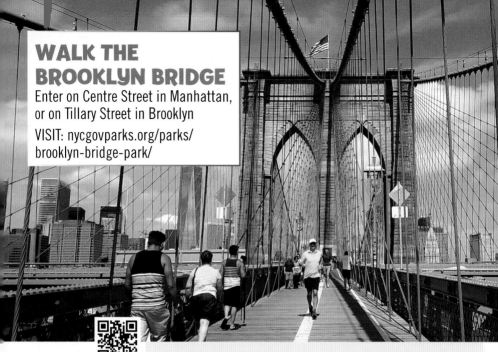

WALK THE BROOKLYN BRIDGE

Enter on Centre Street in Manhattan, or on Tillary Street in Brooklyn

VISIT: nycgovparks.org/parks/brooklyn-bridge-park/

ADMISSION
Free

HOURS
24 Hours A Day,
7 Days A Week

HOW TO GET HERE
From Manhattan
Subway:

A C J N R Z
2 3 4 5 6

Bus: M9 M22 M55 X15 M103

From Brooklyn
Subway: A C F N
R 2 3 4 5

Bus: B25 B26 B67 B52 B54 B62

FOR SPECIAL NEEDS
Wheelchair accessible from both sides.

SHELLEY REPORTS

Take a breathtaking one-hour walk across this famous bridge to marvel at its unique engineering and to experience the dazzling New York City skyline.

- **WHERE TO START** Whether you start from Manhattan or Brooklyn, this is one of the most famous walks in the US. Taking this unforgettable stroll is a great way to explore two different boroughs in one day!

- **LOOK FOR . . .** Stare up at the imposing towers, and marvel at jaw-dropping views from the bridge. The two towers are 159 feet tall from the roadway—that's around 15 stories high!

- **PLACES TO VISIT** After you cross the bridge, enjoy dim sum in Manhattan's Chinatown, discover street art in Brooklyn's DUMBO neighborhood, or put your toes in the sand at Brooklyn Bridge Park!

SHELLEY'S ACTIVITIES
Walk over a Famous Bridge!

DID YOU KNOW?

In the 1800s, famous circus impresario PT Barnum marched 21 elephants across the bridge!

③ NOW YOU ARE HERE
More Bridges!
See how many other bridges you can identify as you walk!

Check Out That View!
Take several photos of your walk and share them with other family members or friends.

① LET'S GET STARTED

First, visit: nycgovparks.org/parks/brooklyn-bridge-park/

New Places! New Words!
Look up the definition of these words before you go!

- cable
- caisson
- span
- suspension bridge

④ ON THE WAY HOME
Thinking It Over

- Have you seen the Brooklyn Bridge in any movies? Which ones?
- How long do you think it took to build the Brooklyn Bridge?
- Why do you think the bridge is called the "Eighth Wonder of the World"?

② ON THE WAY
Travel Talk

- How do bridges change communities?
- If you wanted to build a bridge, what skills would be important to learn?
- What are some other ways to travel between two places separated by water?

CAREER FLASH The following careers relate to the Brooklyn Bridge. Do you know what each profession does?

- Architect
- Bridge CAD technician
- Construction inspector
- Civil engineer
- Tour guide

Pick careers to research. What skills and education are needed to pursue these careers?

NEARBY ▶ AFRICAN BURIAL GROUND NATIONAL MONUMENT 290 BROADWAY *PAGE 2*
NATIONAL MUSEUM OF THE AMERICAN INDIAN ONE BOWLING GREEN *PAGE 82*

WHALE WATCHING

Riis Landing, intersection of State Road & Heinzelman Road, Rockaway, Queens, (718) 474-0555

VISIT: americanprincesscruises.com

ADMISSION

Children *(under 5)*: Free
Children *(5–12)*: $33
Adults: $48
Seniors *(62+)*: $43

HOURS

Whale watching cruises available May–Nov. Check website for cruise dates and times.

HOW TO GET HERE

Subway: A to Beach 116th Street, then transfer to Q22 or Q35 bus

2 to Flatbush Avenue, then transfer to Q35 bus

Bus: Q22 Q35

FOR SPECIAL NEEDS

The boat is wheelchair accessible.

SHELLEY REPORTS

Yes, there are whales in the Rockaways! Set sail into the Atlantic Ocean for a truly exhilarating adventure as you try to catch a glimpse of these majestic and gentle mammals!

- **BEFORE YOU GO** Wear layers to prepare for brisk weather. Pack sunscreen, a bagged lunch, binoculars, and a camera, and prepare for an unforgettable day searching for humpback whales and playful dolphins!

- **NATURALISTS** There are naturalists on board every whale cruise—they'll share all the amazing facts they know about whales and dolphins, and will provide tips on how to spot them!

- **SEAL AND BIRD WATCHING CRUISES** In March and April, join one of these special cruises to see harbor seals, grey seals, and birds like peregrine falcons, Cooper's hawks, loons, cormorants, northern gannets, and more! Check website for details.

MORE INFO: **ShelleysLearningAdventures.com**

SHELLEY'S ACTIVITIES
A Whale of a Time!

DID YOU KNOW?

Humpback whales each have unique tail flukes, just like human fingerprints!

1 LET'S GET STARTED

First, visit: americanprincess cruises.com

New Places! New Words!

Look up the definition of these words before you go!

- baleen plates
- breaching
- krill
- mammal

2 ON THE WAY
Travel Talk

- Why do some animals migrate from one place to another every year?

- Can you give an example of a food chain in the ocean?

- Why are humpback whales and harbor seals classified as mammals?

3 NOW YOU ARE HERE
Video Journal

Once you spot whales, dolphins, or other animals, take a video. Be sure to narrate the sighting!

Ask a Naturalist

Ask the on-board naturalist questions about the creatures you see—they can offer a lot of interesting information!

4 ON THE WAY HOME
Thinking It Over

- What types of things do humpback whales communicate with the noises they make?

- What human-created threats do whales and other sea creatures encounter in the ocean?

The following careers relate to whale watching. Do you know what each profession does?

- Conservation scientist
- Marine engine mechanic
- Marine research assistant
- Whale biologist
- Whale watching naturalist

What skills and education are needed to pursue these careers?

NEARBY ▶ HISTORIC AIRCRAFT RESTORATION PROJECT 50 AVIATION ROAD *PAGE 46*

SPECIAL EVENTS CALENDAR

Many of the venues listed in this book have recurring or annual special and seasonally themed learning advenures and celebrations. Please check the venue website listed in the book to get more information.

JANUARY

American Museum of Natural History	Butterfly Conservatory
Central Park	Winter Jam
National Museum of the American Indian	Winter Blast
New York Botanical Garden	Holiday Train Show
New York Hall of Science	Gingerbread Lane

FEBRUARY

African Burial Ground Monument	Black History Month
American Museum of Natural History	Butterfly Conservatory
BAMkids	BAMkids Film Festival
Intrepid Sea, Air & Space Museum	"Kids Week"

MARCH

African Burial Ground National Monument	Woman's History Month
American Museum of Natural History	Butterfly Conservatory
Lincoln Center	Young Music Makers
Teatro SEA	World Day of Puppetry

APRIL

American Museum of Natural History	Butterfly Conservatory
Lincoln Center	Big Umbrella Festival
New York Hall of Science	Science Playground and Mini Golf
Roosevelt Island	Cherry Blossom Festival
Prospect Park	Earth Day Celebration

MAY

Central Park	Shakespeare in the Park
City Island	Memorial Day Parade
Intrepid Sea, Air & Space Museum	Fleet Week
New York Hall of Science	Science Playground and Mini Golf

JUNE

Central Park	Harlem Meer Performance Festival
New York Hall of Science	Science Playground and Mini Golf
Prospect Park	Celebrate Brooklyn Festival!
Socrates Sculpture Park	Queens Green Day

JULY

Governors Island	NYC Poetry and Children's Poetry Festival
Louis Armstrong House Museum	"Hot Jazz, Cool Garden"
New York Hall of Science	Science Playground and Mini Golf
Prospect Park	Celebrate Brooklyn Festival
Queens County Farm Museum	Thunderbird Mid-Summer Pow-Wow

AUGUST

Louis Armstrong House Museum	"Hot Jazz, Cool Garden"
National Museum of Mathematics	NYC Math Festival
New York Hall of Science	Science Playground and Mini Golf
Pregones Theater	BX Summer Block Party
Prospect Park	Celebrate Brooklyn Festival

SEPTEMBER

Bronx Zoo	Boo at the Zoo!
Governors Island	NYC Unicycle Festival
Historic Richmond Town	Richmond County Fair
Intrepid Sea, Air & Space Museum	Space & Science Festival
New York Hall of Science	World Maker-Faire
Queens County Farm Museum	The Amazing Maize Maze
Transit Museum	Bus Festival

OCTOBER

American Museum of Natural History	Butterfly Conservancy
Bronx Zoo	Boo at the Zoo!
BAMkids	Bamboo! Halloween Celebration
Central Park	Pumpkin Flotilla at Harlem Meer
Historic Richmond Town	Pumpkin Picking

NOVEMBER

American Museum of Natural History	Butterfly Conservancy
Brooklyn Museum	Brooklyn Children's Book Fair
New York Botanical Garden	Holiday Train Show
New York Hall of Science	Gingerbread Lane
Transit Museum	Holiday Nostalgia Rides

DECEMBER

American Museum of Natural History	Butterfly Conservancy
New York Hall of Science	Gingerbread Lane
New York Botanical Garden	Holiday Train Show
Transit Museum	Holiday Nostalgia Rides

WEBSITES

After you've explored these 75 learning adventures, I know you'll be eager and excited to explore more amazing places and activities including:

CHESS

CHESS FORUM
chessforum.com

MARSHALL CHESS CLUB
marshallchessclub.org

FAMILY PERFORMANCE VENUES

ALVIN AILEY
alvinailey.org

DANCE THEATRE OF HARLEM
dancetheatreofharlem.org

FLUSHING TOWN HALL
flushingtownhall.org

THUNDERBIRD AMERICAN INDIAN DANCERS
thunderbirdamericanindiandancers.
wordpress.com

MARKETS

BROOKLYN FLEA MARKET
brooklynflea.com

QUEENS INTERNATIONAL NIGHT MARKET
queensnightmarket.com

MUSEUMS & COLLECTIONS

CITY RELIQUARY
cityreliquary.org

MOSSMAN LOCK COLLECTION
generalsociety.org

NATIONAL JAZZ MUSEUM
jazzmuseuminharlem.org

THE AKC MUSEUM OF THE DOG
museumofthedog.org

MUSIC & THEATER JUST FOR KIDS

JUSTKIDDING: SYMPHONY SPACE
symphonyspace.org

STORY PIRATES
storypirates.org

PARKS, PLAYGROUNDS, & GARDENS

BROOKLYN BRIDGE PARK
brooklynbridgepark.org

VESSEL AT HUDSON YARDS
hudsonyardsnewyork.com/discover/vessel

WAVE HILL
wavehill.org

SCIENCE

WORLD SCIENCE FESTIVAL
WorldScienceFestival.com

SHIPS & BOATS

PADDLE THE BRONX RIVER
bronxriver.org

PIONEER SCHOONER
southstreetseaportmuseum.org/Pioneer

RED HOOK BOATER'S
redhookboaters.org

ROCKING THE BOAT
rockingtheboat.org

STADIUM TOURS

CITIFIELD
mlb.com/mets/ballpark/tours

YANKEE STADIUM
mlb.com/yankees/ballpark/tours/classic

TRAMPOLINE, TRAPEZE & ZIPLINES

ALLEY POND ADVENTURE COURSE
www.nycgovparks.org/programs/rangers/
adventure-course

BROOKLYN BOULDERS
brooklynboulders.com

FLY HIGH
flyhighNY.com

ACKNOWLEDGMENTS

I love this guide!

Our mission was to give parents, guardians, and teachers the tools to help support children in the learning process, to encourage and support parental involvement, and to foster the partnership between school, home and community.

Thank you so much to Ron and Steve Sussman of Sussman Education/Lightswitch Learning for having the extraordinary wisdom and vision to introduce teachers, parents, and students to these unique and engaging New York City learning adventures.

A huge thank you to the wonderfully talented graphic designer, Paula Jo Smith, for her brilliant layout and design and the countless conversations we had to ensure we had it just right!

An enormous thank you also to my publisher and editor Adam Reingold. I could never have done this without you. Your wise counsel, guidance, and sensational editing inspired us all and helped us cross the finish line!

—Shelley
New York City, April 2019

INDEX

PHOTO CREDITS